— PLAN A —
LIFE
YOU LOVE

A WOMEN'S GUIDE
TO HEALTH, WEALTH AND HAPPINESS
WITHOUT LIMITATIONS

HANNA OLIVAS

KIM CALLINAN I LENA KHAIS I SYLVIA BECKER-HILL I PRUDENCE HATCHETT I SHEREE WERTZ
STEPHANIE DAUBLE I BETHANY KLACO I MP MONTIGNY I TRISH GLEASON

Table of Contents

INTRODUCTION

"Plan a Life You Love and Live It Out Loud" is not just a book; it's a collective journey of ten passionate souls, including yourself, coming together to share their wisdom, insights, and experiences on how to craft a life filled with purpose, joy, and authenticity.

In this transformative anthology, each coauthor pours their heart and soul into revealing the keys to unlocking a life of fulfillment and meaning. From navigating career transitions to cultivating meaningful relationships, from overcoming adversity to embracing self-love and self-care, these ten voices offer a rich tapestry of wisdom that inspires, empowers, and uplifts.

Through heartfelt anecdotes, empowering affirmations, and actionable strategies, "Plan a Life You Love and Live It Out Loud" invites readers to embark on a journey of self-discovery and transformation. With each turn of the page, they are encouraged to dream bigger, reach higher, and dare to live life on their own terms.

Whether you're seeking guidance on finding your passion, creating a vision for your future, or stepping boldly into your power, this book serves as your trusted companion on the path to living a life that sets your soul on fire.

So, dive in, dear reader, and let the wisdom of these ten extraordinary souls ignite the spark within you. It's time to plan a life you love and live it out loud – because your dreams are worth pursuing, your voice is worth amplifying, and your life is worth celebrating.

Hanna Olivas

Founder & CEO of She Rises Studios

https://www.linkedin.com/company/she-rises-studios/
https://www.facebook.com/sherisesstudios
https://www.instagram.com/sherisesstudios_llc/
www.SheRisesStudios.com

Author, Speaker, and Founder. Hanna was born and raised in Las Vegas, Nevada, and has paved her way to becoming one of the most influential women of 2022. Hanna is the co-founder of She Rises Studios and the founder of the Brave & Beautiful Blood Cancer Foundation. Her journey started in 2017 when she was first diagnosed with Multiple Myeloma, an incurable blood cancer. Now more than ever, her focus is to empower other women to become leaders because The Future is Female. She is currently traveling and speaking publicly to women to educate them on entrepreneurship, leadership, and owning the female power within.

PLAN A LIFE YOU LOVE AND LIVE IT OUT LOUD

By Hanna Olivas

Early Years

Where it all began…When I sat down to write this book I felt I needed you to know not all of my life was planned; in fact, a great deal of it was filled with unimaginable pain and suffering. As you begin to read this, it is my hope that you will be open-minded about the intimate details shared. I poured my heart and soul into this because I want you to know that you can still plan a life you love no matter your age, past, or circumstances.

I always knew I wanted to be an entrepreneur, even before I could spell or say the word correctly. I had my first experience as a business owner at the mere age of nine when I opened my very own lemonade stand, and from there, it bloomed. My next venture was starting my own babysitting business. Mind you, this was back in 1987 when life was—what I consider to be—much simpler than it is now.

As a proud Latina, I knew that my journey would not be without its unique challenges. In a world where being a woman already came with its set of hurdles, I, as a Latina, often found myself navigating through additional layers of prejudice and stereotypes. The glass ceiling wasn't just a metaphor; it was a tangible barrier that I had to shatter, piece by piece.

Growing up, I faced judgments and biases that questioned my capabilities solely because of my gender and ethnicity. But I refused to let society's misconceptions define me. I realized that breaking the glass ceiling wasn't just about personal success; it was about paving the way for other Latina women to rise with me. I made it my mission to be a voice for change, to challenge the norms that limited our potential, and to stand in solidarity with every woman striving to overcome adversity.

However, when I was younger, I never thought I would be a victim of sexual assault. I always felt that I was invincible, that nothing wrong could ever happen to me. That all changed in the blink of an eye at a very young age. I was sexually molested by my mother's boyfriends at the ages of two and three years old, in my teens, and again by my ex-husband.

"Stop, I can't breathe. You are hurting me." These words I spoke at the young age of four. I begged many times, saying these exact words to a man who stole my innocence repeatedly.

"Mommy, it hurts down there." "Mommy, help me." "Please, Mommy, I'm sorry."

As I write this chapter, I am reminded of every ounce of pain I endured and had to relive again until I was eight. Every bath he gave me, every time he held me down, every time he used his hand or objects, I prayed to God to take me away. Every time he touched me, he took a piece of me away. I was his target, his focus, and his obsession. I felt dirty, scared, violated, and alone. I had no idea what to do or how to stop it. I only knew it felt wrong, and it hurt.

From a young age, I experienced sexual abuse, molestation, and later on, domestic violence. These experiences left me feeling disconnected from love - both from others and within myself.

The abuse finally stopped but the pain, physically, mentally, and emotionally, continued. In fact, at times, I can still smell his stench and feel his touch as if it were happening now. I often have to remind myself that it's no longer happening. I am safe and loved; I am on a healing journey.

It's hard to describe the feelings I experienced in the aftermath of the assault. I felt violated, ashamed, and completely alone. I didn't tell anyone what had happened for a long time, not even my closest friends or family. I thought it would go away if I just pushed it down and tried to forget about it. But it didn't. It lingered like a dark cloud hanging over my head.

Throughout the years, I felt marked as if the whole world knew I was this dirty little girl.

Physically, he caused long-term problems from the sexual abuse. I had to heal from second and third-degree vaginal tearing. I was anxious and depressed and suffered from years of night terrors and panic attacks.

I was afraid to be alone, afraid of bath time, fearful of the dark, and scared of men. I operated in total fear. I carried this into my young teenage years straight into adult womanhood. I was a guarded, dirty, damaged girl. I was so angry at my mom, dad, and grandparents for not protecting me. In fact, I grew a pure hatred for them and the man who violated me.

As the years went by, I became rebellious, promiscuous, hateful, and careless. I didn't care if I lived or died. I wanted the pain and memories to stop. But they just wouldn't. I became a runway and was eventually taken by the juvenile court system and held for long periods of time.

I questioned God, faith, and people in general. I had no trust in myself. I wasn't given the option for help or therapy until I was 14, and by then, I didn't want it or understand how it could help me. I was permanently marked and damaged goods.

I always wondered, "Why me? Why anyone? Why does this type of evil exist in the world?"

Unfortunately, I wasn't a Me Too victim just once. I was raped at the age of fourteen by someone I knew and again by a man whom I married at a very young age. It hurts my heart deeply to even write this because it's so unbelievably hard to fathom. All the abuse and rape I suffered finally stopped at the age of 21 years old. You can imagine how messed up I was. Two of my beautiful children are a product of years of forced rape.

Now, I was a young mother who had no idea how to even take care of myself, let alone two children. At this time, I was always operating in fight or flight mode, and I finally reached out to the one person I thought would help me - my mother. I called and asked her, "Can I please come home?"

Her reply was cold and so detached. She said, "No," and hung up the phone.

It was then and there that I realized I would never again be a victim!!! But I was wrong. I had no idea how to start, but I knew I needed to get the hell out of the marriage I was in and away from his darkness.

What a struggle it was to break the chains I was bonded by.

For the first time since I was a little girl, I prayed for God to give me the courage to fight back and leave for good. I escaped with my two young children and nothing else. I had to start over from scratch. I was terrified on so many levels. But I knew if I didn't leave, I would always stay a victim.

Little did I know that was just the beginning of more heartache. I thought by escaping my last perpetrator I'd be free. But I wasn't, and in fact, he made my life so difficult. I became even more depressed, and a downward spiral effect happened. I had lost custody of my children and my mind, body, and soul.

I was so angry at the time that I'd lost my children and even more angry at how they'd suffered at the hands of a man who forced himself on me over and over. I remember how sick I was from the stress. I ended up in the hospital often for panic attacks, unexplained illnesses, rashes, hair loss, and more. I spent years fighting and trying to heal, live, and see my children. It wasn't until years and thousands of mistakes later that I would see my children and finally be their mother again.

Healing

As someone who has experienced trauma, I understand the deep and lasting effects it can have on self-perception, self-worth, and the ability to love oneself. The profound impact of sexual abuse, molestation, and domestic violence shaped my view of myself and made self-love feel like a foreign concept. It took time for me to recognize how these experiences had influenced my beliefs and behaviors. Understanding the impact of trauma is crucial to begin the healing journey.

All those years as a victim and barely surviving. Most days, I felt numb and ashamed. The fragile glass had finally been shattered. I remember one day asking myself, "Will it get better than this? Will I survive all these years of mental, physical, and sexual abuse?"

"How do I fix my shattered life? Does anyone out there love me? Am I safe?"

The answer is yes, but it wasn't going to be easy. I finally made a choice to seek help.

I remember going to my first therapy appointment. I kept saying to myself, "I won't share it all. They will think I'm crazy." The truth is, I wanted to share everything that happened to me, and in my first appointment, it all came out like vomit.

I spent years in therapy, church, and prayer. I also spent years running from myself, making more bad choices in life and men. I just wanted to be loved and healed. When would it be my turn? I became a mother two more times in my journey.

It wasn't until the birth of my youngest son that it all changed. As I was leaving the hospital, I remember thinking I was shattered but not broken. It was time to pick up the pieces and start healing once and for all. I wanted to be a better mother, and I wanted to be able to breathe.

Let's talk about faith first. Being a victim of sexual abuse, I often questioned, why me?

"Why would God allow such evil and devious acts to happen to one of his own children?"

The answers came in waves. We all face trials and tribulations; however, it's what we do within the storm and what we learn from it that matters. There were many times that I spent nights alone in tears, asking God to take me, to make the pain and abuse stop. I spent years being sexually molested and abused. I felt dirty, marked, and damaged beyond repair. I was constantly living in fear and anger. From time to time, I would feel as if there was a glimpse of hope ahead for me.

I always have said and believed, "The faith of a mustard seed can turn into a garden of hope, healing, and opportunities." Faith is an incredible gift we are all born with. We just have to develop our faith and know that we are not defined by our circumstances, and we can begin a new life healed, happy, and healthy. Part of healing from trauma also requires forgiveness of ourselves. Sometimes we blame ourselves for what happened and believe we caused it, which is not true.

The perpetrator is the person responsible for the abuse; we've done nothing to deserve that. I hope you realize that in your healing journey. Most would say it's impossible to forgive such an act and the person who carries it out. However, in order to heal, we must forgive ourselves and focus on how to move forward.

I went back to therapy and church. I joined women's Bible studies. I did everything I could to heal. I worked two, sometimes three, jobs to survive and care for my children as a single mom. I earned everything through handwork. I bought a car, we lived in a tiny apartment, and we had food, water, and electricity. I did the very best I could with the means I had.

One day, I was in church, listening to the pastor speak on forgiveness. The kids were in youth group, and I was in service alone, listening to his message. How we must learn to forgive if we want to be forgiven. I thought to myself, "Fuck that. I want the men who hurt me to suffer." Oh, I was so angry. I thought, "How can a pastor say this? Does he know what I've been through? Are you seriously saying I have to forgive the men who stole my innocence, years of my life, and years of pain?"

When the service was over, I immediately grabbed my kids, and I left, angry.

How can anyone forgive those things? Why do the perps get to be forgiven? Months went by before I stepped into the church again, and as soon as I did, a woman from Bible study asked if we were ok. She hadn't seen us for a while. I told her yes. She asked why we were absent, so I told her the truth. Again, it all came out like vomit.

This woman began to cry, and she reached out to embrace me with the warmest, safest hug I'd received in years. For the first time ever, I felt safe. It was definitely a day I'll never forget. She then asked if she could pray with me, and I agreed. Hearing her prayer amazed me; it was like she knew my every hurt, thought, and fear.

From then forward, I went to church and women's groups, continued therapy, and really focused on how to forgive the unforgivable. Every day has been a work in progress. I lived the first thirty-seven years of my life in fear, anger, judgment, regret, unforgiveness, and more.

I believe and know what kept me fighting and trying was my children. Their love for me was greater than any pain I'd experienced. They showed me forgiveness, unconditional love, and just how beautiful life could be.

Once I realized how to ask for help and how to open up, I began to heal. I learned that I was shattered but never truly broken. Thank you to the woman at church for not seeing me as the marked, dirty girl but for seeing me as a woman and mother who wanted more for herself and her children.

Even with all of the support, I still felt like I was stuck. I was stuck in the trauma of what had happened to me, and I didn't know how to move forward. That's when I decided to seek out therapy. It was a hard decision, but it was one of the best decisions I have ever made. I could confront the trauma through therapy and begin to work through it.

It wasn't easy, and sometimes I felt like giving up. But I kept going, and slowly but surely, I began to see progress. I started to feel like myself again like I could move on from what had happened to me. And now, years later, I can confidently say that I am healed. I am still a work in progress, but I am no longer defined by the trauma that once consumed me.

Every step I've taken since that day has been to heal and forgive. I can truly tell you no one should bear this burden alone. If you have been the victim of sexual abuse, please, please speak up. Tell someone who can help you!! There is help out there, I promise you. Don't keep silent. Scream out for help. Whisper if it's unsafe but let someone know.

Since I began my healing journey and completed years of therapy, I now travel and speak to other women. I teach them to use their voice. How to speak up, how to leave, or even escape. To know they are not alone.

Healing is a word that is used so often, and I wonder if people realize and understand the actual meaning and how to become fully healed. Especially when the hurt or damage is so deep within. As you read this chapter, I pray you find your inner peace and healing. I have found my healing comes from three places, Faith, Forgiveness, and Love.

One of the most important steps in my healing process was acknowledging and validating my experiences. For years, I had suppressed my pain and emotions, denying the impact they had on me. However, by acknowledging the truth of what I went through and allowing myself to feel the pain, I created a safe space for self-reflection and acceptance. It was a challenging process, but it allowed me to validate my own experiences and recognize that what happened to me was not my fault.

It wasn't until the Me Too movement gained momentum that I began to feel like I could talk about what had happened to me. Watching other women come forward with their stories made me feel less alone, giving me the courage to speak out. I wrote a blog post and book about my experience and was overwhelmed by the outpouring of support that I received from friends and strangers alike.

I am here as your Me Too But Never Again Warrior. You are not alone. You are loved and worthy. To those reading this book who've Never experienced sexual abuse or trauma like this, please educate yourself and look around. Be the voice and advocate for those who can't.

If there's one thing I've learned on this journey, it's that healing is possible. It's not easy and takes time, but it's possible. And if my story can inspire even one person to seek help and begin their healing journey, it will have all been worth it. Me too, but never again.

Personal Growth

One significant aspect of my healing journey was reclaiming my personal power. I realized that the trauma I experienced did not define my worth or identity. It required a conscious effort to develop resilience, set healthy boundaries, and redefine the narratives I had about myself. Through therapy and self-reflection, I began to recognize my strengths, talents, and inherent worthiness. It was a transformative process that allowed me to regain control over my life and cultivate self-compassion.

Over the years of my healing journey, I know three things to be true: Faith, Love, and Forgiveness go hand in hand. As I've written my second *Me Too But Never Again* book, I've grown so much, and I no longer feel like that marked, dirty girl. I live a beautiful life and have a wonderful family and support system. Although my abusers were my mother's boyfriends, a teenage friend, and my ex-husband and father of my children, I can genuinely say I have let go and moved past so much of the pain. That's what I want for you. Please, never give up on your healing or yourself. You are worthy and loved. You are not alone. Speak out and tell your truth. Find the support system that works for you. Don't be afraid to tell!

The concept of self-love was something I struggled with for a long time. But as I began to heal, I learned that self-love goes beyond superficial notions. It involves practicing self-care, accepting myself as I am, and showing compassion towards my imperfections. Mindfulness became a powerful tool, allowing me to stay present, appreciate myself, and practice positive self-talk. Embracing self-expression through various outlets, such as art or writing, also played a vital role in nurturing my self-love.

When I finally saw myself in a positive light, it was like love at first sight. The moment I recognized my own beauty and the goodness within my heart, I fell in love with who I had become. Each and every day, as I wake up and look in the mirror, I see the reflection of someone I genuinely love and cherish. It has been a long and challenging journey to get to this point, but every step, every tear shed, and every moment of self-discovery has been completely worth it. I am grateful for the growth, the healing, and the transformation that has brought me to this place of self-love.

During my journey of discovering self-love, I came to realize that a significant part of it was having faith in myself, even during moments when I couldn't see, feel, or hear the difference it was making. There were times when doubts and insecurities crept in, making me question if this path of self-love was truly worth it. But deep within, I had an unwavering belief that I deserved love and that cultivating self-love was crucial for my well-being. So, even when progress seemed slow or imperceptible, I remained faithful to my journey. I held onto the belief that with time, patience, and consistent effort I would experience a transformation that would bring me the self-love and acceptance I longed for.

Throughout the ups and downs, I stayed committed to my path of self-love. It wasn't always easy, and there were moments when I stumbled or felt discouraged. But I refused to give up. I reminded myself that self-love is a lifelong journey, and the results may not always be immediate or tangible. I trusted the process and the small steps I was taking each day, knowing they were building the foundation for a healthier and more fulfilling life. My faith in myself and the power of self-love fueled my determination, allowing me to persevere through challenges and setbacks. As I look back now, I am grateful for staying faithful to my journey because it has led me to a place of self-love and empowerment that I never thought possible.

Oftentimes, I found myself tempted to revert to my old ways, to slip back into patterns of self-destruction that I had grown comfortable with. It was as if there was an internal battle between the familiarity of my past and the desire to truly love myself. But I recognized that surrendering to those old patterns would only perpetuate the cycle of self-destruction, and I would have to start the journey of self-love all over again. It was a sobering realization that pushed me to break free from that destructive pattern once and for all. I made a firm commitment to myself to focus on rebuilding my self-love, refusing to let setbacks deter me from my ultimate goal.

Let us shift our focus and dedicate ourselves to rebuilding our self-love once and for all. It's time to break free from the cycle of starting over and make a lasting change. We owe it to ourselves to break the pattern of self-destruction and embrace a path of self-empowerment. By consciously choosing self-love every day, we can rebuild ourselves from the inside out and create a foundation of self-worth and inner strength that will withstand any challenges that come our way. It may not always be easy, but with determination, perseverance, and a steadfast commitment to our own well-being, we can transform our lives and experience the true depth and beauty of self-love.

My journey was a testament that we can transcend the noise of prejudice and stereotypes by embracing our uniqueness and turning it into our greatest strength. Together, as a united force, we shattered the glass ceiling, proving that our voices, stories, and resilience are powerful catalysts for change.

When we open up and share our journey and allow others to be a part of it, it helps us heal and face the hardest days. It helps us to purge and renew and, most of all, it helps us to realize that we're not alone.

Dealing with Loss

My most pivotal moment was overcoming the loss of my unborn baby, Mario. I was eight and a half months pregnant when I lost him. I had been preparing for this miracle baby to come into my life. I was so excited and shocked because I didn't believe I could have more children, and in your forties, being told you're going to have a baby is mind-blowing.

As my husband and I prepared for this little baby boy to enter our lives, I started having complications. He wasn't growing inside properly. Doctors told us he may just be a small baby. I was having breathing issues, anemia, and pain, and eventually, we were told I had Lupus.

Which was a major misdiagnosis. We ignored all the signs and continued to prepare.

We decorated a nursery for him, had a baby shower, did the 3D ultrasound to see the sex of the baby, and took maternity pictures; we did it all. I was glowing and growing, or at least I thought I was. The dreadful day came when I lost our child. I felt like the biggest failure in the world. I couldn't even bear to look at my husband. All I saw was how broken-hearted he was and how I was the cause.

I thought, "My stupid body, my stress, me me me, I did this!" I took the blame for it all. I hated myself. How could I do this to us? I went through the pain of losing him and the funeral service, but all I could think of was how much I failed myself, my baby, and my husband. His nursery sat untouched for months. I couldn't take the pain of going in there. I was so angry with myself, God, and the world.

I had full hatred take over. The loss totally devastated and changed me. I disappointed my husband, my family, and my friends. I walked in shame for almost a year. I hit major depression and began drinking to hide the pain. I wanted to be numb.

I couldn't get out of bed. I wouldn't even look at myself in the mirror or even shower or brush my hair. I felt a deep darkness and despair. I didn't eat or sleep for months. All I knew and felt was heartbreak and pain. I was a failure. I wanted my sweet baby. I wanted to hold him and kiss him. I needed him with every ounce of my being. He was my sweet baby.

I was still having issues with breathing, pain, anemia, insomnia, digestive issues, extreme fatigue, and the feeling of doom. I didn't care; I just kept going down this black hole. Finally, my husband gave me a choice, live or die, but do something! It was then it hit me so hard. Hearing the pain and frustration in his voice and the words, "Live or die, but do something, make a choice!"

I was so angry at him for not being more sensitive to my loss. What I didn't realize was that he had lost Mario too, and now he was losing me.

This also affected my children who were watching their mother slowly disappear. For days, I kept replaying his words over and over.

At the time, my middle daughter was living with us, and she hadn't been feeling well, so I took her to the store to buy something to help her nausea. I'll never forget this moment as long as I live. We are standing in the aisle about to buy Pepto and crackers, and it hit me! I said, "Jasmin have you had your period ?"

Her reply was, "No, Mom, I'm always late."

I said, "You're not late. You're pregnant!" She laughed. I said, "Humor me, let's get a test, the Pepto and crackers." So we went home, she tested, and boom, it said positive!!! Right then and there the choice for me was clear, I chose to live! I was going to be a grandma. I was so excited.

I felt this immediate sadness lifted off me. I went into my room and cried out, "Thank you, God, for this blessing and second chance." I vowed then and there that I would let go of my own pain and disappointment and be the best wife, mom, and grandmother I could be. I struggled, but I wasn't going to let anything stop me from healing and living. I was going to be the best grandma ever!

I began going to church, therapy, praying, and journaling. I started exercising, eating healthy, and reading any and everything positive. I started to feel mentally and emotionally better, but not physically. In fact, I felt worse. I went to doctors again, explaining my symptoms, only to be told it was stress and grief. As time went on, we welcomed the most beautiful baby I'd ever seen. My little Dominic Mario. My heart was full, and he instantly became my world. The loss I felt of losing my own child subsided. I began to focus on him and only him. I was so thankful for this baby for so many reasons. I felt a void being filled daily.

The Diagnosis

Yet, I still wasn't healing physically. I became worse. So I went to a different doctor this time, and he ordered tests, imaging, and other things. After all was said and done, it took eight months and four doctors to discover I had a rare blood disorder and cancer.

I was faced with a major diagnosis that would forever change my life. They believe that is why I lost my child. Talk about more heartache and pain for me, my husband, my children, and now my grandson. I felt utter rage at the diagnosis and being told there was no cure was hard to deal with. I left the doctor's office, ran to my car, and cried out, "Why, why now?"

At that moment, I felt defeated again. The drive home was a blur. I still, to this day, don't remember how I got home. What I do remember is telling my husband and him responding, "You have a choice; fight to live or die trying."

Can you imagine hearing those words? But he was right! I had to fight to live and be here. That was the day (May 28th, 2017) that I made a choice to Unleash my power! I chose to live! I chose to fight with all my power. I chose to forgive myself, let go of the pain of losing my baby, and let go of the pain of the diagnosis. I chose myself for the first time! I wanted to be free of my past, loss, and pain. I wanted to create a new life no matter what it took. I refused to accept this diagnosis or let the loss of my baby set me back. I believe when I truly let go of it all and realized a lot was out of my control, that is when I Unleashed the power within me to control only the things I could.

I had to have faith and trust that God would make a way and guide me. Even though I have this illness, I have made it my life's mission to live a life without limits. I've made a decision to be free and let go of what I cannot change. I use my power in other ways. I've embraced all that I am. I have forgiven myself and look forward to the future.

At first, I had a ton of pity parties and blame games. One of my personal limiting beliefs was, "I am not good enough," or "I'm scared." It took me three decades and a terminal illness to realize that I was the very person hindering my growth, my life, and my future.

That was a tough one for me to swallow. After being diagnosed with terminal cancer, I had to completely change my life, my mindset, and my entire world. I needed to find balance and peace and learn to accept the diagnosis yet continue to do what I loved daily.

Then, someone who made a huge impact in another community reached out to me and said, "You are not alone." She used her influence to create one of the largest communities for Multiple Myeloma. It was then I knew my messy diagnosis would be my biggest message. Unfortunately, she passed away from Multiple Myeloma, but she left a legacy behind for many others and made so many changes in the cancer community. She used her influence for good.

The day before she passed, I was in New York City sharing my journey on the Tamron Hall show, and she called me shortly after, telling me how proud she was of me and how I had to promise to keep her legacy alive. She wanted me to continue sharing my story and help others know they are not alone. She asked me to never give up and always do good.

She was an influencer of love and hope. She helped thousands upon thousands of men and women diagnosed with blood cancer.

From the last call we had together upon her passing, I promised her never to stop doing good and being a voice for others who couldn't.

Despite my symptoms and how I feel physically and emotionally, I wanted to "Become An Unstoppable Woman!"

I am a wife, mother, grandmother, daughter, sister, and friend. After that devastating news, I made my mind up and NOTHING would change it. I began to learn, shift, and find the willingness to grow into a new mindset and lifestyle.

I began to face genuine fears and phobias; I began to forgive, and I began to be forgiven. Life will forever look different to me. I had to come to the hard truth—that I was simply existing—but how do I live without limits?

Here is my answer. Up until writing this very chapter, I can tell you how absolutely amazing this journey has been. I refused to just lay down and give up.

I have to be intentional from the time I rise till the time I sleep. I have to stay focused. I rise daily with the expectation of abundance, love, peace, health, amazing relationships, and a zealous will for life. I never take one day for granted or the people in it.

Many have asked me, "How do you live knowing you are terminally ill?"

My answer is simple: "I am dying to live, not living to die."

As women, we face many adversities, struggles, heartaches, loss, depression, health issues, financial ruin, and more. It's how we handle some of these inevitable issues that matter. So, build your mindset, tenacity, and perseverance muscles. Break Through Before You Break Down. Begin and end your days knowing and believing you are Unstoppable.

You are authentically and beautifully you.

Rise Up, Lead, Live, and Enjoy being the Everyday, Unstoppable Woman that I know you can be and already are!

I strongly encourage you to find a mentor or coach to help you develop your skills, muscles, and strength in this journey. Wake up early. Set goals; stay on task. Read books that fill your mind with positive and creative value. Get organized.

Write down on paper what you want your life to look like. Design it and live it. Does this all sound scary to you? Maybe a little overwhelming? It's not, I promise.

Continuing to Strive for More

I was confident, ambitious, and driven, which showed in everything I did. But deep down, I have always battled a hidden enemy that threatened to derail everything I worked so hard to achieve: self-sabotage.

Self-sabotage is a common problem that affects many people and can take many forms. For me, it has been a constant, nagging voice in my head that tells me I'm never going to be good enough, that I don't deserve success, and that I am destined to fail. I often set ambitious goals for myself only to sabotage my own efforts through procrastination, self-doubt, and negative self-talk.

My self-sabotage became a serious problem when I was approached by a potential client who wanted me to take on her large project. It was a high-profile opportunity that would have been a significant coup for my business, but as soon as I received the proposal, I felt a sense of dread wash over me. I began to question whether I could deliver the project, whether I had the expertise and resources to handle it, and whether I could manage the pressure and stress that would come with it.

As the days went by, I became increasingly anxious and overwhelmed, and I found myself procrastinating and avoiding the work that needed to be done. I started missing deadlines and failing to follow through on my commitments, and my confidence crumbled. I knew that if I didn't get a handle on my self-sabotage, I would lose the client and risk damaging her reputation. Fortunately, I realized that I needed help and sought a therapist specializing in helping people overcome self-sabotage. Through a series of sessions, I began uncovering the underlying beliefs and fears driving my self-destructive behavior. I learned to recognize the negative self-talk and challenge the limiting beliefs holding me back.

I began to practice self-compassion and self-forgiveness, learning to be kind to myself and let go of past mistakes and failures. I started to focus on my strengths and accomplishments rather than dwelling on my shortcomings and failures. I learned to set realistic goals for myself and to celebrate progress along the way.

As I continued to work on myself, I found that my self-sabotage dissipated. I started to take on more challenging projects with confidence and enthusiasm, and I could deliver exceptional results. I no longer felt like a fraud but rather a competent, capable professional who was worthy of success.

Today, my business is thriving, and I have a reputation as a skilled and reliable expert in my field. I have learned to recognize and overcome my self-sabotage, and I am now passionate about helping others do the same. I speak at conferences and events, sharing my story and insights with others struggling with self-doubt and negative self-talk.

Businesses and Growth

As a teenager, I always had a passion for travel and for beauty. After high school, I moved to California to pursue a career as a freelance makeup artist. It was then that I realized I didn't want to work for anyone but myself. But I needed training in makeup, and training cost money. So, I worked as a waitress to pay for my schooling and to attend one of the best makeup academies on the West Coast. Once I graduated, I began to work in the fashion and beauty industry. I traveled, worked with celebrities, and loved making women feel and look beautiful.

After 25 years in the industry and four children later, I felt I was missing out on my true calling and purpose. So, it was time to unplug and regroup. I opened a few different businesses in events and marketing before going back to owning my makeup line and shop. But I still had this feeling, this void. I knew I loved working with women and helping others; what I didn't know was that it would lead me to open She Rises Studios in the middle of a pandemic.

One day, I started journaling and making a vision board, and before I knew it, I had filled it with hundreds of goals and dreams. One of them was to have my own TV show for women. I wanted to inspire women to be the best versions of themselves. Another dream was to open a shelter for battered women and children. I wanted to help women heal. I began to see a pattern developing. "How do I make this dream a reality?" I asked myself over and over.

Finally, one day, I was sitting with my oldest daughter, and it just hit me like a train. I told her, "We need to start a network for women!!" That day, She Rises Studios was born. At first, it started with simple Facebook and Instagram pages filled with inspirational quotes that we had written.

I remember us sitting across from each other, day in and day out, trying to decide just what She Rises Studios was meant to do. We decided to step out in faith and host a podcast. Neither of us had any experience in podcasting, so we decided to take a class at our local library. Next thing we knew, we were podcast hosts for the She Rises Studios Podcast!

All I can say is wow! We invited women we knew to speak on topics and share their life experiences. It was all so exciting. Within the first three months, our podcast became syndicated. We were featured on all the major podcast platforms including Spotify, iHEART Radio, iTunes, and more.

We started with zero capital and a whole lot of faith. Now our podcast is one of the most sought-after women's empowerment podcast shows in less than a year with no investment, no experience. Just faith over fear and a dream turned into reality. During all of this, we worked countless hours, made mistakes, lost sleep, and shed tears. But through it all, we never gave up. We learned and we lost, but we never failed.

Now, here comes the good part. Just six months into our podcast, again sitting with my daughter, I told her, "We should write a book in collaboration with other like-minded women." I remember the look on her face; it kind of makes me laugh thinking about it now.

Less than 16 months later, She Rises Studios had become a podcast, TV show, publishing company, and academy, and we've expanded into the United Kingdom as well. I was just a girl with a dream and a passion. That dream became a reality. So, if you have a true desire to become an entrepreneur, step out in faith; don't wait for the right time. Just do it, even if you have to do it afraid.

I have always wanted to be a successful businesswoman, running my successful, multi-digital media firm for women entrepreneurs. I was confident, ambitious, and driven which showed in everything I did.

Of course, I too had setbacks. I often set ambitious goals for myself only to sabotage my efforts through procrastination, self-doubt, and negative self-talk.

As I continued to work on myself, I found that my self-sabotage dissipated. I started to take on more challenging projects with confidence and enthusiasm, and I could deliver exceptional results. I no longer felt like a fraud but rather like a competent, capable professional who was worthy of success.

Today, my business is thriving, and I have a reputation as a skilled and reliable expert in my field. I have learned to recognize and overcome my self-sabotage, and I am now passionate about helping others do the same.

I continued to share my story on the Today Show, People Magazine, NewYork Post, LA Times, and in about another hundred-plus interviews. I traveled the country speaking in English and Spanish, sharing my story. My audience grew, and people were following my story and getting involved with the blood cancer community.

It's not the me show, it's the we show—where we stand together to make a difference in our communities, families, and businesses for causes we believe in and so much more.

That is why I created She Rises Studios. I wanted to help educate, empower, celebrate, and elevate women globally. In March 2020, so much changed forever when the pandemic struck our world as we know it. So many lives lost, jobs gone, homelessness, and other terrible issues. I wanted to help and saw the need in women who were in survival mode. I told my daughter, "We have to do something."

Since then, we have helped hundreds of women become six and seven-figure income earners by becoming women entrepreneurs. We offer educational services and platforms for women to be seen and heard.

I used my influence for good and my mess for a message. I didn't want to stop there. I wanted to see a difference in the level of care for patients. Our medical care in Nevada is terrible. We are understaffed, there are no specialists for Myeloma patients, and most have to travel to California for treatment like myself.

Can you imagine traveling to another state while being sick and on chemo for weekly or monthly treatments and the expenses and stress? I needed to see that change, so I started reaching out to our local legislation asking for specialists, treatment centers, and any support we could get. Most didn't care or listen. However, the few who did listen helped me grow the non-profit and raise money to bring more advocacy and awareness to Las Vegas.

We started supplying hospitals with toys for pediatric cancer patients and their families, and we began hosting events to raise money to help families pay their bills while fighting off cancer.

I opened up a non-profit organization called the Brave and Beautiful Blood Cancer Foundation in my own hometown community to help families who'd been stricken by a blood cancer diagnosis. We supply care packages and food as well as co-pay assistance, travel to chemo and doctor's appointments, and emotional support groups. To date, we've served well over 2500 Las Vegas families who've been affected by cancer.

It became a movement here, and we've raised almost $1 million to date! That has helped so many families. To many, one million isn't much. But I personally saw how this helped hundreds of local families.

I didn't want to stop there. I wanted to do more.

The non-profit continues to serve our local community and grow, and I love it! I used my influence for good. Yes, I still battle cancer today and will be on lifelong treatments, but I will never stop fighting or give up! I will do even more to help others fight too.

Our platforms consist of podcasts, TV shows, public relations, and publishing for women. We've helped over 200 women become national and international best-selling authors in just two short years. It's a true community of extraordinary women who use their influence for the greater good. She Rises Studios is now in over 20+ countries, helping women be seen and heard and helping them establish successful businesses to sustain themselves and their communities.

Moving Forward

I keep telling myself, "Go Mama go, yes, you can have it all." Every day I wake up and repeat this over and over in the morning. My day usually begins at 5 am. Yep, this mama is a 5 am club mama. I love to use the first few, quiet hours of the day for prayer, meditation, journaling, exercise, or just playing some music to get me pumped.

Being a mom and an entrepreneur takes balance, coffee, prayer, and skill. Mostly coffee and prayer. As soon as the 8 am alarm sounds off, it's go time. My little nine-year-old Sophia is up and at 'em. I have learned that keeping the two of us on a morning schedule and routine keeps us from going crazy. It sounds silly, but it's true. It seems like together we are a morning comedy show. I get her to school, and I have calculated precisely how many hours of work I can get done before she is out of school. I call this "time blocking," or time management.

Now here is where the word "unstoppable" comes into play. No matter what life throws at me, I remain hyper-focused on my unstoppable mindset and clarity to get me through the day. Because sh#t happens and we, as mothers, need to be prepared and able to juggle balls, bananas, apples, and lemons, all while standing on one foot. Can you picture this? I hope so because it happens daily. Did I mention yet that I am also the proud wife of an amazing man I've known for thirty-five years? So yes, while being a mother of five children ages nine to thirty, a wife, and a hot grandma to my amazing grandsons, I am also an Unstoppable Mompreneur.

Now, let's talk about when sh#t hits the fan and days don't go as planned. I can't even count how many WTF moments I have on a daily basis.

What should I do? How do I react to the school calling to pick up my sick daughter, not being able to meet a deadline for a client, or if I get sick?

The answer is that life happens to us all, and we, as mothers, tend to want to fix everything and carry the burden of the world on our shoulders. However, obviously, that's impossible! So what I say is, "It's ok…" We are humans, not robots. We don't have control over everything, but we do have control over how we react to it. My gift when sh#t hits the fan is laughter. I simply chuckle and tell myself, "It's OK, Mama," because you can still have it all.

Keep going; don't quit. Be still and let life's storm pass. Give yourself the grace to pick up the pieces, and Go Mama Go! This is my mantra in life and business. Always find humor and laughter; it heals any situation. I want you to know that no mompreneur is perfect. We all juggle, we all make mistakes, and we all lose our balance at times. That's just life. We all look up at the sky and say "Really? Like, why now?" That's ok mama, keep going, laughing, and chucking it in the chuck-it bucket.

A limitless life meant I had to persevere and believe in myself despite any and all circumstances. The process is not overnight—it's building your resilience and determination muscles. But it also means living in gratitude at all times.

So, build your mindset, tenacity, and perseverance muscles that will make you mentally stronger to get through the tough days swiftly. Break Through Before You Break Down. Begin and end your days knowing and believing you are Unstoppable. Because you are.

All moms have a magical power within. We kiss owies and they go away. We wipe away tears and turn them into wishes come true. We manage to be in two places at one time. We always smile, even when we want to cry. We are the first ones to rise and the last to sleep. It seems we have an unending amount of energy— or so our children believe.

Being a mother is truly one of the biggest blessings of my life. I have five children, and each child is so different and requires a different magical power from me. For example, my middle and youngest daughters require my patience power. As I sit here writing this, I laugh because it's so true. My oldest son requires me to use my communication magic because he is an onion— it's one layer at a time with him. My middle son requires my sensitivity and magic power because he feels everything. My oldest daughter is my diamond in the rough, and she requires my intuitive magical powers. She keeps everything in.

As I describe to you my five children and the magical powers I use, I realize no matter how old they are, they will always want and need their mom and my magic.

Every day I wake and dash to my sexy coffee machine. I bet you thought I was going to say my husband. Nope! It's coffee. The smell of my first morning cup brings me joy. As I sit and drink the cup of what I believe is magic, I pray, read, and meditate. I love my mornings of gratitude and solitude. Every mama needs her alone time— end of discussion!

After I finish my morning ritual, the siren sounds at approximately 7 am. This is when we move fast. Get the kids up and ready, pack lunch, drop them off at school, and hope I haven't forgotten anything this time.

As soon as they're off at school, I am off to run my company. Time for a different magic hat. I have a team of approximately fifteen employees, and each one of them requires a mom superpower. Sometimes—or most times—it's patience and communication. I typically work nine hours a day, five days a week, and I try to do the balancing act most days. But let's be real, this requires skill and talent.

I say this because I haven't even begun to discuss my wife magic. Yup, it's a thing. My hubby, whom I love dearly, also needs love, attention, affection, and a wife who is present, who listens and gives understanding. One who knows his quirky ways and needs.

How the hell do I manage all this and not lose my shit one hundred times a day? Well, the truth is I do lose my shit or have at least one WTF moment a day! I'm not going to pretend any of this is easy because being a mama is like being a warrior at times. I'm often on the battlefield of laundry, dishes, and sticky stuff.

When the WTF moments happen, that's when I call my mama and she uses her magic to calm me. Thank God for moms, right? Who knew having children was like a combo of the George Lopez Show and Family Feud?

Most days, I get through with laughter and coffee. However, there are days when I need to refill my magic cup before it runs out. As a mama, we must always take care of ourselves first. Yup, you heard me! It's not being selfish, so drop the mom-guilt now! Before you can help your children, you must take care of yourself. How and when is up to you. I usually take a mom day on Sundays and do whatever I want. I read, journal, and love a good facial or massage. I also highly recommend yoga because it gives you that inner silence we need most. I make sure my kids, grandkids, and hubby give me the space I need to replenish what I have used. And yes, hubby gets his alone time too. He goes fishing or golfing often, and even after so many years of marriage we still date each other with a date night or two.

There is so much that goes into being a mom, wife, and grandmother. It's never-ending. One of the greatest gifts of being a grandmother is seeing those sweet faces, spoiling them rotten, and returning them to their parents with lots of sugar and loud toys. Payback!

I believe mom magic is real, and it's incredible! To be able to create a tiny little human and watch that human go through life is one of my most cherished things in life. Seeing my youngest to oldest thrive and grow into incredible adults is so amazing.

I always say, "Damn, I'm good." I raised my kids to be kind, loving, hard-working, and giving children. My grandkids are the same way. I am truly blessed beyond measure. Is it all picture-perfect? Nope. Are there days when I've wanted to give up? Yes—but I can't imagine life without them.

"Plan A Life You and Live It Out Loud" seems like a simple statement and concept. I have recently found myself looking forward to planning so much more, from the simplest things to the grander and everything in between. It excites my soul to know I have the ability and freedom to plan and live it. I've had to learn I cannot control everything, but I can plan. Life is filled with possibilities and opportunities for every human being. Sometimes we're afraid to take them or see them. We can get caught up in routine instead of just being. However, if we prepare and follow the plan on those days when we get caught up in the mundane of routine, we can look at the plan as a reminder that we must live out loud.

Now, as I've mentioned, I was almost born right into trauma from a young age. That I didn't plan. I knew somewhere in my heart that I loved business and wanted to own one, but I didn't have a plan. I am a mother of five, and none of them were planned. I have cancer and definitely did not plan that! Here's where the planning began. When you are faced with illness, your perspective changes. Mine certainly did! I started being very intentional about how I spent my time and with whom. I love to travel and have planned and gone on the most extraordinary adventures. I am present daily in all I do. I live for every moment and plan as much as possible, and then I do it. I don't focus on how; I focus on the why. I've never been more happy in my life and loved myself as much as I do now.

Even though it may have come from tragedy it doesn't have to end in it. Plan your moments and live them boldly. Don't forget how amazing your life and value are. Be bold, and embrace every opportunity. There is so much I didn't plan, but the things I have planned truly outweigh the negatives. Life is beautiful; business is amazing. I am grateful to share my journey with you! Live your life so loudly that the galaxies far away can hear your joy! Say yes to you, to your business, your health, and your wealth. Become a limitless human being.

Xoxo,
Hanna

Kim Callinan

President & CEO of Compassion & Choices

www.linkedin.com/in/kimcallinan
https://www.facebook.com/kim.callinan/
https://www.compassionandchoices.org/about-us/leadership-board-committees/senior-leadership

Kim Callinan is an accomplished non-profit leader, motivational speaker, and expert in organizational management, cultural intelligence, and end-of-life care. With over thirty years of experience, she has been instrumental in initiating integrated campaigns for social change. Her leadership of Compassion & Choices, the nation's premier non-profit organization advocating for patient-directed end-of-life care, exemplifies her ability to inspire and motivate others toward realizing meaningful change. As a prominent figure in the end-of-life care movement, Kim presents at conferences, community events, legislative hearings, and policy briefings. Her unique experiences with individuals courageously facing their mortality have profoundly shaped her perspective. These encounters, marked by intentionality and resilience, underscore the importance of embracing life's transient nature and preparing for its conclusion. Kim's dedication to sharing these insights forms the core of her work. For a deeper understanding of Kim's journey and Compassion & Choices, visit www.compassionandchoices.org.

WISDOM FROM THE BRINK:
LESSONS FOR LIVING A MORE MEANINGFUL LIFE

By Kim Callinan

Last Holiday: A Storyline Resonance

Picture this: It's 2006, and *Last Holiday* graces the big screens, introducing us to Georgia Byrd, portrayed by Queen Latifah with charm and vibrancy. In this heartwarming romantic comedy, Georgia, a seemingly ordinary woman, is jolted by the news of a terminal illness. Faced with a stark timeline, she embraces her limited time, embarking on a luxurious European adventure, living courageously and freely without inhibition.

Real-Life Inspirations: Our Terminally Ill Advocates

While a fictional tale, aspects of this cinematic journey resonate deeply with me in my role at Compassion & Choices, America's leading nonprofit organization championing improved care and expanded options at life's end. As CEO, I've met many individuals like Georgia at the crucial crossroads of their imminent mortality. These real-life heroes, our terminally ill advocates, choose to live their lives fully in the face of devastating diagnoses, demonstrating remarkable resilience. They organize their affairs, let go of grudges, say the unsaid, and forge unforgettable memories with family and friends. While some, with the resources and energy, embark on vacations and travels like Georgia, most simply live with increased clarity and intention, being discerning with their time and ensuring that their encounters are meaningful.

Their commitment extends beyond personal spheres; they strive for meaning, spending their remaining time advocating for societal change. They collaborate with us to educate the public and lawmakers about end-of-life care and choice, using their unfortunate experiences to advocate for much-needed end-of-life policy changes. Many understand that their efforts may not benefit them directly, yet they persist, wanting to do whatever they can to leave a lasting impact on the world, and they do.

The resilience and conviction displayed by our advocates with terminal illnesses are both inspiring and profoundly impactful. With their rare clarity and conviction, some have an effect that defies the odds and transcends the impossible. Take Brittany Maynard, the courageous 29-year-old who moved from California to Oregon to access medical aid in dying. Her decision ignited a national dialogue on the nature of dying, a conversation that persists to this day. Hannah Olivas' struggle with cancer not only raised awareness within the Latin community, as evidenced by her cover feature in *People Magazine Español,* but also helped propel the relevant bill to the Nevada governor's desk, and in time, no doubt, her and others' continued resiliency will remove the final obstacle. John Radcliffe, a lobbyist in Hawaii, played a pivotal role in successfully passing the Hawaii Our Care Our Choice Act, a legislative journey that spanned two decades. His challenging experience in accessing the law led him to champion a posthumously passed amendment, significantly streamlining the process for others and minimizing the obstacles he once faced.

The email exchange below I had with Lynda Bluestein, one of our terminally ill advocates in Connecticut who has since died, is such a perfect demonstration of the incredible gifts that these advocates impart to the world during the last days of their lives:

> *Dear Kim,*
>
> *I had PET scans on September 21st that confirmed P.O.D. which is oncologist talk for progression of disease. Not in remission anymore.*
>
> *My oncologist wanted me to start on another course of chemo immediately but I said I needed a month to get my head around*

those pesky metastatic lymph nodes that showed up in the scans. I also told him I wanted to think about Clinical Trials, not because they are in any way curative but because ovarian cancer treatment has not changed in over 50 years and there are new investigations using mRNA, monoclonal antibodies, and immunotherapeutic agents in combination with the standard chemo cocktail.

I have a daughter and granddaughters—plus all the women who have or will have ovarian or Fallopian Tube cancers who could be helped. I am now in the process of interviewing with PI's (principal investigators) at Yale and Memorial Sloan Kettering to see what trials I qualify for, that are open to me, and that I might want to consider participating in.

The clock is definitely ticking. My Yale interview is this coming Friday.

Paul and I have seen several plays and concerts, traveled semi-locally to Boston and upstate NY, and stayed very busy with enjoying the fall leaves and a whole host of museums we've never gotten around to visiting.

Today we are playing bridge at our Duplicate Bridge Club in Newtown, and tonight will be on ZOOM to record an interview again. Life does go on and I am so grateful that I have the opportunity to do something in support of the causes I believe I have a unique position to make a difference.

That's a very long way of saying, I'm still good to go.

Lynda

By observing how they approach life, we all have much to learn. Please join me in seizing a terminal approach to life.

Seize the Day: A Terminal Approach to Life

Consider Nancy Uden from Corcoran, Minnesota. She was diagnosed with glioblastoma multiforme in late 2022. Despite facing an aggressive cancer with a 15-month prognosis, ten months into her diagnosis and treatment, Nancy's outlook remained incredibly positive. "It wasn't until I was told I was dying that I truly began to live," she confided. "I now prioritize time with loved ones and focus on what's essential, like helping Compassion & Choices advocate for legislative change in Minnesota. My diagnosis, in a strange way, feels like a blessing." Nancy's resilience in adversity is as inspiring as any cinematic story.

I often leave their presence and ask myself: Why should we wait for a life-altering diagnosis to begin living purposefully? Why not seize each day with the courage and intentionality that comes with an acute awareness of time's preciousness? What if I lived like I was terminal every day?

These reflections have prompted me to transcend minor irritations, accept or reframe issues beyond my control, and strengthen my relationships. They have fortified my resolve to lead a life of authenticity and bravery, embracing each moment with a renewed perspective on what truly matters. Inspired by their example, I now confront challenges that once seemed insurmountable, invigorated by the realization that true courage lies in facing the seemingly impossible. I've become deliberate about how I spend my time, thoughtfully choosing with whom and on what activities. I have even penned my obituary, aiming to clarify my legacy aspirations.

Enriched by the wisdom of these extraordinary individuals, I am driven to absorb, embody, and impart the invaluable lessons of our terminally ill advocates, aspiring to disseminate their profound wisdom far and wide so others may also draw strength and inspiration from their remarkable journeys.

Embrace Their Wisdom: An Enlightened Approach to Leadership

I am also profoundly driven by the desire to mirror our advocates' courage, intentionality, and authenticity: They deserve leadership as extraordinary as their own. Committed to this ethos, I recently obtained an MBA, secured gerontology, cultural intelligence, diversity, equity, and inclusion certifications, and became a death doula. My pursuit goes beyond formal education; I am deeply engrossed in self-directed learning in leadership, management, and the science of well-being. This includes delving into the teachings and research of renowned experts in positive psychology, such as Martin Seligman, Brené Brown, Laurie Santos, and Angela Duckworth.

Blending Wisdom: Insights from Research and Reality

One day, a profound epiphany struck: The science and evidence championed by academic researchers on well-being and living a meaningful life mirrored the wisdom I was gleaning from our terminally ill advocates; this inspired me to write this chapter. By blending the real-life experiences of those confronting mortality with scholarly insights, I aim to offer a distinct perspective on leading a fulfilling life.

While death is an inevitable part of life, crafting a meaningful existence requires thoughtful consideration and deliberate action. This chapter presents six universal lessons that transcend culture and race, guiding readers toward a more purposeful existence. Having all six lessons in mind might seem overwhelming. However, embracing the perspective that your life is finite can lead to a transformational shift in attitude. This shift can naturally integrate these lessons into your daily living, enabling you to embrace a life marked by courage, intentionality, and a sense of purpose.

Lesson 1: Live in the Moment: Finding Joy and Gratitude in Life

Through my interactions with terminally ill supporters, I have gained profound insights into the value of living in the moment. In the face of their finite time, these individuals embrace every second with a heightened sense of meaning and purpose. They prioritize activities that bring them joy and fulfillment. Amidst their substantial challenges—pain, suffering, endless medical appointments—they exhibit an extraordinary ability to find joy in life's simplest aspects and gratitude for each day they have.

This approach to life, emphasizing the significance of each present moment, is strikingly reflected in Laurie Santos' teachings in her popular course, "The Science of Well-Being," available on Coursera (Santos, 2020). Santos corroborates the idea that recognizing the finiteness of time can lead to a more mindful, meaningful way of living, aligning perfectly with what I've observed in our advocates. Their experiences serve as a powerful reminder of the importance of cherishing every moment we have.

Lesson 2: Letting Go of the Trivial

A critical insight I've gleaned from terminally ill advocates is the art of letting go of what seems essential but is, in fact, trivial in the grand narrative of life. This ability to differentiate and prioritize is a profound skill, demonstrating an understanding that many issues we often regard as significant are, in reality, fleeting and inconsequential.

These advocates tend not to linger on interpersonal disagreements or over-analyze casual remarks. Even substantial mistakes are viewed through a lens of relative insignificance. They often express that at life's end, such matters hold no real value; they neither contribute to happiness nor to the legacy they wish to leave. Their strategy isn't about ignoring problems, but rather assessing their importance in the larger picture. This approach liberates emotional and mental resources, enabling a deeper connection with life's meaningful facets, such as nurturing relationships and pursuing passions.

The principle that "what you focus on grows" is particularly relevant here. Giving attention to concerns, even through simple acts like discussing or complaining about them, magnifies their presence in our lives. Conversely, by not fixating on these issues, they are effectively minimized.

This phenomenon is not just anecdotal but is grounded in academic research. Cognitive Behavioral Therapy, a well-established psychological approach, posits that focusing on manageable and positive aspects of life, rather than obsessing over every problem, can significantly reduce anxiety and enhance overall satisfaction. This idea is further supported in positive psychology, especially in the works of Martin Seligman. His research underscores the value of concentrating on personal growth and relationships over material or superficial achievements.

In his book *Whale Done!* Ken Blanchard applies this principle to management theory, illustrating how focusing on positive behaviors rather than problems can lead to better outcomes. Similarly, Richard Carlson's *Don't Sweat the Small Stuff...and It's All Small Stuff* advises letting go of minor issues, further echoing this sentiment.

Thus, the lesson from terminally ill advocates is poignant and clear: The power to discern and release even seemingly important concerns can open the door to a more tranquil and rewarding life. This insight reminds us that what may appear to be crucial often loses its significance when viewed against the backdrop of our entire existence.

Lesson 3: Manage Anxiety and Emotions

A notable characteristic I have observed in our most powerful terminally ill advocates is their ability to manage their anxiety and emotions effectively. Many have described themselves as reformed control freaks and spoken about the fact that accepting that they were dying forced them to recognize that so much of life is uncontrollable. It became too overwhelming to attempt to control everything, so they ultimately had to give up the idea that they could control life and instead focus their energies elsewhere.

The importance of focusing on controllable aspects of life to manage anxiety is also highlighted in well-known literature. A pertinent example is *The 7 Habits of Highly Effective People* by Stephen R. Covey. Covey emphasizes the significance of proactive focus on what one can influence, a principle that resonates with the practices of the advocates I've encountered. They embody resilience by concentrating on their responses to life's challenges, which is a powerful strategy for emotional well-being and anxiety management.

Lesson 4: Courage as a Path to Meaningful Living

I am always amazed by the courage our advocates demonstrate. I have watched self-reported introverts, who have spent a lifetime fearing public speaking, emerge to become the face of an issue, powerfully speaking to the media, lawmakers, and the public. When I ask them what got them over their fear, their answer is always the same: "I'm going to die in a few months anyway; what do I have to be afraid of?" I have watched some people fall deeply in love; others have difficult conversations they have previously avoided with their loved ones or friends, and almost universally, they all wish they had lived this way sooner.

The courage exemplified by our terminally ill advocates aligns with research on the science of happiness. For example, research by Brené

Brown, who has extensively studied vulnerability and courage, indicates that embracing vulnerability and stepping into the unknown, which often requires great courage, can lead to more authentic and fulfilling experiences. If you have not seen it, I would highly recommend her widely viewed TED talk on vulnerability and courage (Brown, 2010).

Lesson 5: The Power of Resilience in the Face of Adversity: Navigating Dual Realities

A profound strength emerges from observing the resilience of terminally ill advocates like Nancy Udon, Brittany Maynard, Hanna Olivas, and John Radcliffe. It's not merely about steadfastness in adversity, but also their capacity to navigate dual realities: accepting their terminal condition with its accompanying challenges and finding joy in the life that remains. This duality, embracing both the harsh truths of their situation and the potential for positive experiences, exemplifies true resilience.

This concept of balancing acceptance and hope aligns with contemporary psychological research. It suggests that the most resilient individuals can hold space for sorrow, hope, pain, and joy. They do not fall prey to toxic positivity, oversimplifying the emotional spectrum by enforcing relentless optimism. Instead, they acknowledge and accept the complexity of their emotional experiences, embracing both the struggles and the moments of peace and happiness.

This nuanced understanding of resilience reveals it as more than just endurance; it's a multifaceted skill that involves understanding and integrating the range of human emotions. It is about navigating the delicate balance between acknowledging reality and nurturing hope, crucial for authentic engagement with life's challenges and personal growth.

Lesson 6: The Centrality of Relationships and the Need for Belonging

In interactions with our terminally ill advocates, a profound strength and depth in their support systems and communities is consistently observed. As they face the complexities of their conditions, the relationships and connections they cherish often deepen, becoming more meaningful. This strengthening of bonds and communal support provides comfort and underscores the irreplaceable value of close relationships in our lives.

The crucial role of community and relationships in leading a fulfilling life is robustly supported by academic research. In her book *Love 2.0: Creating Happiness and Health in Moments of Connection* (Fredrickson, 2013), Barbara Fredrickson emphasizes how nurturing positive relationships can significantly enhance our well-being. Similarly, Laurie Santos discusses the importance of social connections to our happiness in her popular course, "The Science of Well-Being" (Santos, 2020), available on Coursera.

Furthermore, the fundamental human need for belonging and community is well-documented in psychological research. Susan Fiske's book, *Envy Up, Scorn Down: How Status Divides Us*, (Fiske, 2011) explores how social relationships and the need for belonging shape our behaviors and well-being.

These insights collectively affirm the observations among terminally ill advocates: Supportive, close relationships and a robust sense of community are central to our overall life experience. They highlight that the relationships we forge and maintain, especially when enriched by cultural understanding and a sense of belonging, are indispensable to our well-being and happiness.

Lesson 7: Purpose and Legacy: The Core of a Fulfilling Life

A recurring theme among our terminally ill advocates is their desire to make a meaningful difference in the world with the time they have left. Numerous advocates have expressed gratitude for the opportunity to contribute, finding purpose and significance during a time when so much seems to be slipping away. This desire for impact and meaning aligns with modern psychological research, which continues to build on the foundations laid by Viktor Frankl's theory of finding meaning and purpose as central to a fulfilling life (Frankl, 1946). Modern research supports this, like Emily Esfahani Smith's book *The Power of Meaning: Finding Fulfillment in a World Obsessed with Happiness* (Smith, 2017).

For our terminally ill advocates, this sense of purpose often crystallizes into a focus on legacy—what they will leave behind and how they will be remembered. This is not just a concern for those facing mortality; it's a powerful exercise for anyone. Engaging in legacy planning— thinking about and documenting the impact you wish to leave on the world—is a profound step toward living a purpose-driven life. It helps to clarify your values and goals, providing a compass for courageous and intentional leadership.

Considering one's legacy is not just a theoretical exercise; it's a practical tool for aligning daily actions with long-term intentions. It encourages a shift from passive existence to active life-crafting, where every decision and action contributes to a broader narrative of personal and communal impact.

Thus, I encourage you to reflect on your legacy. What do you want it to be? How do you want to be remembered? It's only with clarity about the impact you wish to make that you can truly lead with courage and purpose. It's an exercise that's beneficial and essential for anyone aspiring to live a life of significance and fulfillment.

Conclusion

As Dr. Laurie Santos highlights in her "Science of Well-Being" course, understanding the principles of happiness is one thing, but the real challenge lies in actively applying them. Knowing what should make us happy is straightforward, yet consistently acting on that knowledge is often more difficult. In my role with Compassion & Choices, I am constantly reminded of this through the extraordinary examples set by our terminally ill advocates. Their intentionality and courage in the face of life's ultimate adversity are not merely inspiring but a daily call to action.

Their presence and actions continually reinforce that living a meaningful life goes beyond understanding—it requires active engagement and deliberate choices. In a way, they act as my accountability partners, their approach to life serving as a stark reminder of the importance of seizing each day. It's an implicit challenge to complacency, pushing me to embody the same purpose and courage they display.

This leads us to a vital question: How can we, too, hold ourselves accountable for living courageously and intentionally? Adopting a terminal mindset can be a powerful motivator to focus on what truly matters. It involves regular reflection on our lives, ensuring we live each day with purpose and intention. This is your invitation to transcend the ordinary and embrace a life marked by purposeful living and joyful engagement with the world.

Bibliography

- Blanchard, K., Lacinak, T., Tompkins, C., & Ballard, J. (2002). *Whale Done! The Power of Positive Relationships*. New York, NY: Free Press.
- Brown, B. (2010). The Power of Vulnerability [TED Talk].

- Carlson, R. (1997). Don't Sweat the Small Stuff...and It's All Small Stuff.
- Duckworth, A. (2016). Grit: The Power of Passion and Perseverance. Scribner.
- Fiske, S. (2011). Envy Up, Scorn Down: How Status Divides Us. Russell Sage Foundation.
- Fredrickson, B. (2013). Love 2.0: How Our Supreme Emotion Affects Everything We Feel, Think, Do, and Become.
- Frankl, V. (1946). Man's Search for Meaning.
- Grant, A. (2021). Think Again: The Power of Knowing What You Don't Know. Viking.
- Santos, L. (2020). The Science of Well-Being [Online Course]. Coursera.
- Seligman, M. E. P. (2002). *Authentic Happiness: Using the New Positive Psychology to Realize Your Potential for Lasting Fulfillment.* New York, NY: Free Press.
- Smith, E. E. (2017). The Power of Meaning: Finding Fulfillment in a World Obsessed with Happiness.

Lena Khais

Founder & CEO of Atlas Paradigm
Manifestation Coach

https://www.facebook.com/groups/lifebydesignforbusinesswomen
https://bit.ly/Lena_Khais
www.atlas-paradigm.com

Lena Khais is a seasoned mindset coach dedicated to guiding individuals on transformative journeys by demystifying manifestation. With a passion for unlocking the mind's potential, Lena empowers people to attract the life they authentically desire. Her unique coaching approach blends neuroscience, spirituality, and humor, creating an engaging and effective method for personal growth. Lena specializes in harmonizing gratitude, conscious intention, and practical steps to offer a comprehensive approach to manifestation. As a highly sought-after coach, she inspires numerous individuals to overcome limiting beliefs and take control of their destinies. Contributing to the book "Plan the Life You Love," Lena shares insights on the power of gratitude, the art of visualization, and practical strategies to transform desires into extraordinary reality. Through her coaching and writing, Lena continues to make a positive impact, influencing others to align their thoughts and actions to their soul's purpose for a journey of abundance and fulfillment.

PARADIGM SHIFT: LIFE BY DESIGN

By Lena Khais

"We don't attract what we want; we attract what we are"
—Kathleen Cameron

Introduction: The Power of Manifestation

"What is your biggest manifestation win?"

"Did you ever manifest winning the lottery?"

"What is the craziest manifestation experience you've had?"

When people find out that I am a manifestation coach, they immediately have a dozen questions for me. And I absolutely love it! The best part is that I never have to repeat the same story twice, because once we harness the power of manifestation, every day brings new "wins." So, to answer those questions in order:

1. The life that I live by my design
2. I did
3. Watching my daughter manifest visiting Hogwarts and seeing her make friends with two fellow students while waiting on the 9 ¾ platform

But enough about me. Do you know Jim Carrey's story? Before becoming a famous actor, he wrote himself a check for $10 million. To make it "real," he dated it five years in the future. From that point on, he would consistently visualize himself receiving this amount for his acting. Guess what? In 1994, he played in *Dumb and Dumber* and was paid exactly $10 million.

Oprah Winfrey is another famous figure who attributes her success to the principles of manifestation. Growing up poor, Oprah faced enough challenges that could have become blocks, dramatically boxing in her life. Fortunately for her, she picked up the habit of consistent visualization, which kept her focused on her goals. She has spoken about creating vision boards that included images of popular television hosts, picturing herself in their shoes. We all know the outcome.

What these stories have in common is the secret recipe for a successful manifestation. But before we get to that part, let's make sure we're on the same page, pun intended, about what manifestation is: Manifestation is attracting into your physical reality what you first create as a blueprint in your mind. Imagine that you're the architect of your destiny, carefully sketching out the reality you would love to live. It is different from daydreaming; it's a purposeful creation of the life that aligns with your desires.

Wow, you say. This sounds really amazing. And, dare I say, pretty easy. But how do I learn how to manifest? What if I told you that you knew how to do it all along? This is actually one of your default "factory settings," along with feeling happy and living your desires out loud. In fact, I think the reason you picked up this book to begin with is that you had a funny feeling that it was the answer from the Universe to your long-standing question—how can I live the life I love? The "aha" moment here is that you do not need to learn it. You just need to remember it. If this makes you feel a certain way, it's probably because you got used to living your life by default. What if I showed you how you can live your life by design, using the power of your mind to focus on the desired end scene and attract it into your physical reality?

I believe that you would agree that everything starts with a thought. If you look at what you have on right now, I bet dollars to donuts it began with you first choosing an outfit in your mind based on your plans for the day. Then you walked to your closet and got those items to put on. You have manifested your outfit. Something that began as an image in your mind turned out as a combination of those clothing items in your physical reality.

You've probably manifested some bigger things, too. Have you ever taken a beach vacation? It all started as a thought, just a dream in your mind. You pictured yourself enjoying the sounds of the waves, the breeze on your face, and your toes in the sand. Then you took some actions, like booking a flight and paying for a hotel. As a result, you got to enjoy the breeze on your face while digging your toes into the sand and listening to the sounds of waves. Congratulations, my friend. You manifested your trip to the beach. The only reason you didn't think of it as a manifestation is because you have been doing it subconsciously for most of your life. Imagine if you master how to do it consciously and intentionally! You can learn to attract what you would love and make it come to life through the power of your mind.

The science behind manifestation

Does it sound a lot like magic? Actually, there is some science to it. Think of manifestation as uncovering the hidden powers of your mind, especially the part that works behind the scenes—your subconscious. It acts as a command center, helping to navigate and guide your thoughts, although you may not even realize it. You probably already know that everything is energy. What you think and feel sends out signals to the universe, and in return, similar things come back to you. It's like placing a phone call. As long as you have the right phone number and correctly dial the digits, you will connect to the person who owns that phone number. It works the same way with your mind. Your thoughts and emotions release a frequency, and the universe responds by aligning circumstances and opportunities that match that frequency.

This is a powerful universal process that is based on the magnetic nature of our thoughts and emotions. At its core is the principle that the energy we emit into the universe—whether positive or negative—draws similar energies and experiences back to us. Do you know what that means? Our thoughts, feelings, and beliefs are energetic vibrations that literally attract the reality that matches that frequency. Take notes. Your thoughts matter! If you keep a positive mindset and allow yourself to feel the excitement of your goal achieved, you align your energy with the frequencies of experiences you wish to attract. On the other hand, dwelling on negativity or doubt inadvertently draws unwanted circumstances into your life.

Your subconscious mind plays a key role, acting as a bridge between your conscious desires and the Universal forces at play. It is a translator, making sure your thoughts and feelings sync up with the energy around you. As you master manifestation, understanding and harnessing the power of your subconscious mind is the key to unlocking the doors to the life you desire. It is like entering the settings into your life's GPS, making sure every thought and feeling points you in the direction you want to go.

Overcoming limiting beliefs

So, is the path from what you desire in your mind to your end scene in a physical reality a speedy highway? Not exactly. We all have limiting beliefs that can act as roadblocks on the manifestation journey. Picture them as little road detours that take you away from your desired destination, or at least delay your trip by taking you off the shortest path. It might even be the scenic route that you end up on that offers you a bundle of learning experiences, but nevertheless—it is not the shortest path to your life's desires.

Common limiting beliefs are thoughts like, "It's not possible for me," "I don't have what it takes," or "It's too late for me to change." These beliefs, often rooted in past experiences, create static in the frequency you're trying to give off. Just like getting the "faster route is available" message on your car's GPS, overcoming limiting beliefs is a crucial step in unlocking the full potential of manifestation. When you navigate the manifestation highway, consider it an opportunity to clear away those limiting beliefs, making way for a shorter and more direct route to your dreams.

One effective technique for tackling limiting beliefs is becoming aware of a thought that may no longer be serving you and questioning it through a series of whys. For example, when you feel like something is out of your reach, ask yourself why. Your answers will most likely help you uncover at least one limiting belief. Write it down and challenge it by questioning where it came from and how it started, and then explore alternative, empowering perspectives. If you look at it from a different angle, it may surprise you how fast it can lose its power over you.

Another great technique for getting rid of ineffective thoughts is positive affirmations. They play a huge role in reshaping your mindset. These self-created, encouraging, present-tense statements counteract the limiting beliefs and displace them from the plane of your mind. Developing a simple and short positive statement that counters your limiting belief is a solid step to dismantling the power of that limiting belief over your mind. The key is to commit to it, be consistent, and allow yourself to feel the feeling of that affirmation being true for you. When you get that little zing in your heart whenever you write it down or say the affirmation, you know that you have begun to truly embody it. Say it out loud as many times and for as many days as it takes for you to believe that it is true.

Lastly, embrace a growth mindset. The goal is not perfection but creation. And when you create, it can't really be right or wrong. So much in this world is really neutral. It is only through our perception and interpretation of a situation that we give it meaning. This is why words matter. If instead of feeling "stuck," you can see it as an opportunity to find alternatives—you transform yourself from the role of a victim into the position of a person who commands the situation and chooses outcomes to your liking. Neither you nor your life is a mistake that requires fixing. As a creator, you have the complete freedom to design your life and make changes to it as many times as you want. By implementing this and other mind-shift techniques with dedication and consistency, you'll gradually remove limiting beliefs, creating space for the abundant and empowering mindset that is key for successful manifestation.

The role of gratitude

Got it, you say. I actually figured that the lingering memory from kindergarten of when Jonny called me a poopy head was just a small limiting belief that should not have defined my self-worth or my perspective on how people see me. Now, with that realization under my belt (no, that belt doesn't make you look fat)—what's next?

Let's explore the importance of gratitude in the manifestation process. Picture gratitude as the magic wand that amplifies your manifestation power. When you express gratitude, you're sending a powerful signal to the universe that you appreciate and are open to receiving the positive aspects of your life. Gratitude shifts your focus from what you lack to what you already have, creating a magnetic pull for more of what you want. Imagine it as a warm embrace from the universe, saying, "I see and hear you; here's more of what you desire."

As a manifestation coach, I highly recommend that you add gratitude to your daily routine. Keeping a gratitude journal by your bedside is a wonderful way to wrap up your day, reflecting on everything that went right for you. Nothing is too big or too small. I promise you that as you start writing it down, you will surprise yourself with how many positive moments you can recall that would otherwise disappear in the fast waters of your running mind.

Gratitude is not only about being thankful for what has already manifested; it's about anticipating the future, creating a magnetic pull for the desired outcome. In fact, I am going to share with you one tip that will change your life forever. If you choose, it will change your life immediately, from this exact moment: Begin expressing gratitude for things you do not yet observe in your physical reality. See, because your mind can't tell the difference between what's imaginary and what's reality, if you consistently express gratitude for what you would love to have in your life but simply don't yet have at your fingertips, the Universe won't have any other option than to deliver to you your desire in a physical form. Where your attention goes, the energy flows. If you focus on what you would love to have, whether you observe it or not, but fill your heart and mind with excitement and appreciation of having your goal achieved, you literally channel the energy to manifest your dream into reality.

Setting intentions

Let me share with you a recent example from my personal life. When my daughter was turning 14, she asked for an "experience" birthday instead of presents. She wanted a glam night on the town for her and three of her friends, complete with a limo ride and a dinner at a nice restaurant. At first, both my husband and I laughed it off. She paid little attention to our skepticism and continued to talk about how excited she was to walk out of the house and see a white stretch limo in our driveway. Slowly but surely we started considering that what she was asking for could be a simple equivalent to what previously would have been a party at home with a bunch of gifts, many of which were just marginally wanted. As I was going down the list of local limo services, she was happily texting with her girlfriends, planning the outfits. I can't lie, for a time I felt a bit uneasy because all of the places I called were renting limos for a minimum of three hours and looking for more than half a grand in payments. That was certainly way beyond what we intended to spend. Once again, she remained focused on her vision, describing to us in detail a selfie photo session they would have before driving off to dinner. She was right. Long story short, I finally found one company that incidentally had a large event cancel and the entire fleet was available for rent by an hour at cost. She ended up having a superstar experience for her birthday and we ended up spending a fraction of what we would normally pay for a traditional sleepover party accompanied by gifts. The moral of this story—where your attention goes, the energy flows. As long as your focus is positive and creative, the energy will be constructive and productive.

What made the limo story come to life was a very well-defined and specific end scene that our daughter created in her mind that was only possible if a stretch limo became available to take her and her friends to her dinner party. When you set clear intentions, it's like drawing a detailed map for the Universe to follow.

By focusing on positive intentions, you shift the energy around you, attracting experiences aligned with your goals. It's like creating a magnetic force that pulls in the circumstances needed for your manifestations to become real. So this is why if you're single and looking for a significant other, you want to focus on all the warm and fuzzy details of your romantic relationship that you would love rather than on a person to date. Or, if you're looking to improve your financial situation, you don't want to keep feeding your current challenges by constantly going over your debts and credit card balances. You want to appreciate everything you already have, however modest it may be in the moment, and picture yourself having more abundance, keeping your focus on positive intentions to attract more resources into your reality.

Visualization

When I say that our daughter saw the limo ride in her mind vividly and in detail, I mean she literally tapped into her visualization skills to play that scenario like a mini movie on the screen of her imagination. You should try it. Close your eyes and picture yourself with your desire achieved—see yourself living the life you would love. It's not just daydreaming; it's a deliberate act of shaping your reality through the lens of your mind.

Visualization acts as a rehearsal for success, allowing you to experience the emotions and feelings associated with achieving your goals. Imagine it as a practice run before the main performance. By consistently visualizing your desired outcomes, you're programming your subconscious mind to align with those visions, making them more likely to materialize. You fine-tune your energetic vibrations to become calibrated to the vibrations of your dream state. If you want to expedite living the life that you love, make visualization a daily ritual, running the movie of your dream on the screen of your imagination, and watch as the universe orchestrates the fulfillment of your desires in your physical reality.

Taking actions

But wait, you say. I already do that but I don't think it is working. Do you know the difference between daydreaming and manifestation? Daydreaming starts and ends in your mind. It is a wonderful activity that has a fantastic ability to elevate your spirit and raise your vibration. But taking inspired actions is what sets manifestation apart and allows you to materialize the blueprint of your desire in the physical reality of your daily life.

While gratitude lays the foundation for manifestation, the importance of taking intentional action steps cannot be overstated. Manifestation isn't a passive exercise of wishful thinking; it is a solid partnership between intention and action. Imagine crafting a blueprint for your dream life—visualization is the ink that outlines the plan, but action is the builder that brings it to life. Each deliberate step you take is a declaration to the Universe that you are an active participant in your destiny. For example, visualizing yourself in a better-paying job is incredibly powerful, but the act of honing your skills, networking, and applying for positions will transform that vision into tangible outcomes. As you embark on planning the life you love, remember that manifestation is a dance between grateful anticipation and purposeful action, where each step moves you closer to the reality you imagine.

Manifestation in different areas of life

The power of manifestation has its transformative impact across every area of our lives, creating a ripple effect that resonates in relationships, career, health, and overall well-being. The beauty of manifestation lies in its overarching embrace. Through conscious intention and aligned action, we not only shape our individual experiences but contribute positively to the world around us, creating a life that resonates with purpose and joy.

For example, in relationships, the power of manifestation operates as a guiding force in attracting authentic connections that align with our true inner selves. By mastering a mindset of gratitude for the wonderful relationships we currently have and envisioning the qualities of our ideal connections, we set the stage for transformative experiences. The energy we send off through gratitude and visualization acts like a magnetic field, drawing people into our lives who resonate with our values and aspirations. Whether it's manifesting deeper connections with existing relationships or calling in new, meaningful bonds, the conscious practice of manifestation allows us to co-create a relationships landscape that brings joy, deep connection, and authenticity.

Let me emphasize two very important points that will forever pivot your relationship to the best possible connection your heart desires. Whether it is romantic, friendship, or a professional partnership, make sure you clearly define the type of interactions, the level of engagement, and the flavor of connections that you desire in a given relationship rather than a generic statement like "I want a boyfriend" or "I want to be married." If we use the example of "I want a boyfriend," you very likely will be presented with an assortment of humans in many shapes and forms with no guarantee of any of those connections maturing into a relationship. After all, you asked for an object—and you will get an object. If you want an experience, like a loving romantic relationship or a supporting professional mentorship, you should be clear about that. Can you tell a difference? So will the Universe.

Another important thing to remember is to always direct your attention to what you would love rather than rehashing what you dislike. The energy flows where your attention goes. If you focus on what you do not like in a given relationship, you will inadvertently attract more of the same. It may sound crazy, but if you think of your experience when you just "woke up on the wrong side of the bed," don't you feel like your entire day is nothing but a chain of unfortunate events? It is because your vibrations are low and slow; you attract lower-level experiences into your physical reality.

Now think about what it means in our pursuit of health and well-being. By expressing gratitude for the present state of our bodies and envisioning optimal health, we tap into the profound connection between mind and body. Manifesting vibrant health involves not only visualizing our wellness goals but also taking intentional steps toward nourishing our bodies and minds. Through mindful choices in nutrition, exercise, and self-care, we actively participate in the manifestation of a healthy and balanced self. The power lies not just in the visualization but in the consistent, aligned actions that contribute to the manifestation of a thriving and energetic self.

Think of a person who is looking to lose weight. If their attention is on the extra pounds that they currently carry on their frame, they approach this goal from the current reality of them being the person who put on the present weight. On top of that, if you think about the power of our words, when you talk about "losing" something, you attest to the fact that you have the ability to find it again. Let's change that.

If you approach the same goal through a mindset shift, you first define the end scene of yourself with the goal achieved. A person who is fit and of a healthy weight acts and lives differently than a person who is in pursuit of dropping weight. First and foremost—you wouldn't be focusing on getting rid of something you already don't have. Simple enough. However, what is more important is all the actions that a healthy, fit version of you lives in your daily life. That version is physically active because it enjoys the flexibility and strength of the body. That version makes healthy food choices because wholesome meals are delicious and make them feel amazing. By shifting your paradigm to the fit version of yourself, you mold your reality into your desired state by taking actions in the image of your goal achieved.

In the realm of career and professional growth, manifestation serves as a beacon guiding us toward a fulfilling and purpose-driven path. Manifestation in career involves not only visualizing professional success but also taking deliberate steps to enhance skills, seek mentorship, and seize opportunities. The alignment of gratitude-fueled intention with strategic, purposeful actions moves us toward a career that resonates with our passions and contributes to our overall life satisfaction. One of the most paramount value-adds here is that by manifesting your desired end state, you focus on your vision of the role that you want to hold rather than attempting to fit the mold of somebody else's expectation.

Finally, manifestation plays a profound role in our journey of personal growth and development. By expressing gratitude for our current state of being and envisioning the best version of ourselves, we set the groundwork for continuous evolution. Manifestation in personal growth involves not only visualizing the qualities and characteristics we aspire to embody but also actively engaging in activities that foster learning and self-improvement. Whether it's acquiring new skills or embracing challenges, the combination of gratitude and intentional action creates a powerful force that propels us toward becoming the individuals we aspire to be, turning us into the authentic, best-self version of ourselves created by our design.

Challenges in manifestation

Despite the transformative potential of manifestation, some challenges may get in the way of the realization of our desires. Earlier, we talked about limiting beliefs and discussed several ways to tackle and remove them. Another common hurdle is the struggle to maintain unwavering faith and positive focus, especially in the face of setbacks or delays. Doubt and impatience can cast shadows on our intentions, disrupting the energy flow needed for manifestation. It frequently comes together with the tendency to fixate on the "how" and "when" of manifestation, rather than surrounding the natural flow, allowing the Universe to orchestrate the details. Overanalyzing the process can create resistance and hinder the natural flow of manifestation energy. You just don't own the "how." You can't control it any more than our 14-year-old could control the cancelation of that large-scale event that resulted in a stretch limo becoming available at a fraction of its usual cost.

Then, there is life. Our busy schedule is full of responsibilities and tasks. Consistency in gratitude practice and intentional actions can be challenging amidst the busyness of daily routines. Distractions, competing priorities, and the demands of modern living may divert attention away from the manifestation journey. Acknowledging and navigating these common hurdles with resilience and self-compassion is an important part of the journey of planning the life you love.

The good news here is you're in control. This is your life that you plan. Navigating occasional life turbulences is inherent to the manifestation process and requires a blend of mindfulness, resilience, and self-awareness. You can do it. Remember what you learned in this chapter. For example, to overcome doubts and maintain a positive focus, practice daily affirmations that reinforce your belief in the version of you with your desire achieved. When faced with setbacks, view them as opportunities for growth rather than roadblocks. It's that paradigm shift. Embrace patience, recognizing that the Universe operates on its own timeline, and surrender the need to control the details.

Here is my final parting gift for you: Learn to balance. Manifestation is a balance between masculine and feminine energies. This has nothing to do with gender. Each one of us is a combination of both. Masculine energy is expressed in doing and taking action. Feminine energy is in embracing the flow and just being. When we lean too much into masculine energy, we white-knuckle our desires and cut off the flow. If you catch yourself feeling this way, think back to the limo story. You will never have all the steps for "how" until after it's done. But you have complete control of "what"—including your vision of you with your goal achieved. Remember, you don't attract what you want. You attract what you are. Go create the life by your design and live it out loud.

Sylvia Becker-Hill

Becker-Hill Inc.

https://www.linkedin.com/in/sylviabeckerhill/
https://www.facebook.com/sylvia.beckerhill/
https://www.instagram.com/sylviabeckerhill/
www.becker-hill.comwww.sylviabecker-hill.com

Sylvia Becker-Hill is a true Renaissance woman, a multiple-published bestselling author, and a seasoned edutainer who has empowered thousands of corporate executives, women leaders, and entrepreneurs around the world since 1997. In 2002, she became the first German coach to earn the coveted title of Professional Certified Coach from the International Coach Federation, establishing herself as a pioneer in the coaching world. Her impressive educational background boasts two university degrees, while her portfolio showcases over 30 certifications in various change modalities, including her accreditation as one of the world's first 10 Certified Master Neuroplasticians in 2023.

Sylvia's mission is to empower you with all the knowledge, tools, and lasting transformation you need to "FLIP" everything that bothers, hurts, or blocks you from living your desires and dreams into unquestionable Freedom, unconditional Love, envisioned Identity, and impactful Power.

Are you ready to discover the joy of feeling unabashedly alive and powerful?

INNER COMPASS CONFIDENCE™
HOW TO FLIP FROM EXTERNAL ORIENTATION TO BEING GUIDED BY SOUL

By Sylvia Becker-Hill

When I was just a little girl
I asked my mother, what will I be?
Will I be pretty? Will I be rich?
Here's what she said to me

Qué será, será
Whatever will be, will be
The future's not ours to see
Qué será, será
What will be, will be

~ Famous lyrics sung by Doris Day on TV
and by my grandmother when I was little.

Confession of a non-planner in a book about planning your life

Maybe it was the bitterness of my grandmother who lost everything during WWII to the Russians and never forgave life for doing that to her…

Maybe it was my mother's overwhelming sense of guilt that she carried around her like an ugly real-fur coat that she hated, yet was too proud to put down…

Maybe it was my father's uneducated, simple brain that was happy to get through a day without being laughed at for saying something stupid…

Maybe it was my German environment which felt painfully heavy, serious, doomed, grey, and wetted by rain all the time…

Maybe it was my secret attitude of defiance that I hid well behind my cute, girlie, fake smile and my sparkless, sad eyes…

… whatever it was, I resisted "planning" for most of my life.

Conditions for planning to work

"Man plans, and God laughs."

~ Old Yiddish adage

1. In order to plan, one must believe that plans have value and will actually help you achieve results
2. In order to believe in planning, you need to believe that you have control over your life and the power to shape it
3. For many, planning is not an instinctive skill; we need to be taught how to make plans and execute them

None of the above was the case for me during the first two decades of my life before I healed my early childhood traumas and accepted being taught planning techniques.

Growing up as an only child in a household scarred by the trauma of war, I became the emotional support for my family, a role known as "parentization." It was powerful yet overwhelming, **leaving me feeling out of control.**

As hard as I tried, I was never able to heal my grandparents' and parents' pain. Only decades later did I learn that no one can make someone else happy. **We have to be our own healers and our own sunshine.**

When I grew up, I didn't think much about the future and never planned. Yet, I did have dreams. As a teenager, I wanted to study in my hometown's famous art academy, then go to Paris and live a bohemian lifestyle in Montmartre.

In my early twenties, I thought I would live my whole life in my German hometown. I imagined living as a childless feminist with lots of lovers, marrying late in my early forties, and making a career as a teaching professor at my university, lecturing about gender studies and art history…

I share this background story to contrast the amazing life I live now, 30 years later:

I am in a bliss-filled marriage with my husband Peter, who is from New Zealand. We have been together for 24 years. We have two wonderful and brilliant sons, despite the fact that, until my early thirties, I thought I would never have children! One is studying sustainable urban design at university and the other is on track to study computer science in the fall. As a family, we love each other deeply and have traveled all over the world, enjoying different cultures and visiting more churches, famous buildings, art galleries, and museums than I can count!

For the last decade, we have made our home in the "Tuscany of the USA," an area of southern California filled with cypress trees, orchards, and olive trees, and surrounded by rolling hills and granite-capped mountains. Our small city has a uniquely pleasant micro-climate, similar to the small areas of the world that have been defined as "blue zones," places proven to nurture optimal health and longevity.

During the Covid lockdown, I finally became a painter, reconnecting with my teenage dream of creating passionate art from a whimsical studio in my backyard that was built from a former children's playhouse under a giant spreading tree. Nearly every evening we have a photo-worthy sunset over the Pacific in the distance. **It truly feels like I live in paradise.**

I have a great circle of girlfriends, locally and internationally on four continents. Our house is freshly renovated and filled with my paintings and originals from artists I know personally. My home is also filled with my biggest passion: books. I have 2,000 books in my library and more in piles beside my bed and in my spacious home office. I have had my own coaching, training, and public speaking business for over 27 years and feel deeply fulfilled by my impactful work showing my clients how to authentically live their best lives.

I didn't plan for any of this. However, it was all created consciously and intentionally, with clear guidance from my soul and 100% trust in my inner compass!

My intentions for this chapter are:

- For you to live a life you truly love
- To empower you by raising your awareness about your relationship with planning and owning your unique planning style
- To give you some contextual framework for understanding the sources of women's common planning sabotage patterns so you can sense those in your life and let go of any guilt or shame about past failed planning
- To point you to the most important "flip" you need to make to empower your planning practice
- To share with you the history of evolving societal planning archetypes as I observed them over the past decades
- To share with you my two core processes for how I create my dream life every day

- To leave you in good faith that you will take enough from this chapter to start growing your own Inner Compass Confidence™ and give you links to get support

Your Planning Power Awareness Questionnaire

"You've probably heard the adage:
'If you fail to plan you are planning to fail.'

Yet only because something is phrased in a clever syntax and quoted by thousands of people doesn't make it true."

~ Sylvia Becker-Hill

Just because I hated the word planning when I was young doesn't mean I don't plan at all. I developed my own very unique style that I'll describe later. For now, I invite you to become conscious about your planning style, skills, and personality by going through the following **Planning Power Awareness Questionnaire**, which will indicate how you tend to approach planning in your life.

I have designed a beautiful journaling chapter with some creative and somatic exercises to deepen and empower your self realization process. You can get our Plan A Life You Love journal where you bought this book as well.

Write down your answers to the following questions as quickly as you can.

1. How do you define planning?
2. Where do you think your definition of planning came from?

3. Describe the relationship you have with planning.
4. How does that relationship show up practically in your life?
5. How much do you plan?
6. In which areas of your life do you plan?
7. What is the time frame of your plans (weeks, months, or years)?
8. Describe the style of your planning, if you have one.
9. How much do you look at your plans, and how do you use them after they are made?
10. Have you been criticized by others for not planning at all, not enough, or not well enough? Or have you criticized yourself with your inner voice about your amount of planning? If yes, how did that make you feel?
11. How well has your way of planning worked for you? If not well, why do you think it didn't? If it works well, why do you think it worked?
12. Have you ever been traumatized by a plan going completely wrong? If yes, what effects did that experience have? How well have you recovered from it?
13. How confident are you regarding your planning skills?
14. Has your relationship with and/or style of planning changed over time?
15. How much do you use the following skills when planning? Write a percentage after the following skills (the total of all your percentages should add up to 100):
    • Thinking
    • Calculating
    • Measuring
    • Intuiting
    • Sensing
    • Feeling
    • Aligning/releasing/healing in preparation
    • Following external advice
    • Using an existing/pre-fab plan

- Internal guidance/principles/beliefs

What did you discover? Did you have any realizations about how you approach planning?

Please reach out to me and share your insights.

From External Influence to Internal Orientation

*"When we perceive ourselves as powerless
and not in charge of our own life, planning feels pointless"*

~ Sylvia Becker-Hill

When it comes to our planning habits and personality, we have many influences:

- Our parents and their planning personalities
- Our family and how they talk (or don't talk) about their plans
- Authority figures such as teachers, professors, and bosses
- Religious beliefs
- Cultural environment and background
- Technological development and tools

In most modern cultures around the world today, patriarchal systems dominate. Patriarchal systems are those where men are considered of higher value than women, and men have more power, status, money, education, work, health care, protection, and freedom.

There is a tendency to forget that, less than 50 years ago, things were very different, gender-wise, from the situation today. As a young girl in

1970s Germany, I heard again and again phrases like, "The most important job for every woman is to find the right husband," and, "Having children and being a good mother and wife is the crown of a woman's life fulfillment." There was little emphasis on the need to learn planning skills because it was assumed that a husband would make most of the life decisions that required planning.

Men of my generation typically had a very different experience. From an early age, they were supported to feel in control of their lives and take on the leadership of others, and they were provided with the tools and training to develop and execute plans to achieve both their goals and the goals of groups and organizations.

Why is it important to acknowledge this gender difference regarding planning, and how can doing so help us women to plan a life we love?

1. We have to be honest about the historic disempowerment of women in order to **discover how to become powerful and free.** If your decisions in life are rooted in the belief that you are a victim of your circumstances and other people are responsible for making the decisions and plans that guide your life, then planning will likely not make sense! Only when you deeply know and experience that you are responsible for your decisions and actions will planning be empowering for you!

2. The historic disempowerment of girls and women has trained us to **automatically look outside of ourselves first for answers** about how we are supposed to live, and how we might plan and achieve goals. But what if **true fulfillment** can only come from our **inner compass?**

3. During the **last 7,000 years**, roads, cities, kingdoms, societies, economies, and financial futures were almost **always planned by men.** This led to planning philosophies and planning tools

invented and designed by men, for men, aligned with their roles and styles of operating and with outcomes that benefited men more than women.

If you ever failed to plan some of your goals or failed to execute plans you made, it might be that one or more of the three reasons above are to blame! Not you, your lack of motivation to plan, or your lack of skills and tools to do so!

The Evolution of the Three Planning Archetypes™

"You can use an eraser on the drafting table or a sledgehammer on the construction site."

~ Frank Lloyd Wright

"All the world is made of faith, trust, and pixie dust."

~ Tinkerbell

"I set an intention and then I listen deeply into my inner depth of silence, following the whispers of my muse and the nudges of my body."

~ Sylvia Becker-Hill

Given the fact that it was kings, war strategists, road surveyors, city builders, architects, and world explorers who historically created the first plans and that the majority of these were men for the last 7,000 years, it is understandable that **the style of planning we were born into is male, intellectual, measurable with number units, and linear** in alignment with the overarching paradigm of our cultural environment.

Excel sheets, project management timeline diagrams, ABC-priorities, SWAT analysis, etc. are born from that paradigm.

The personification of this type of linear, intellectual, fact-based planner is the **archetype of the engineer.** Its advantages are its seeming objectivity, mathematic calculations, clarity, ease of communication, justification in decision-making processes, and scalability for big projects, productions, and corporations.

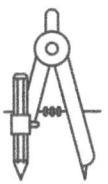 Its disadvantages are its sterility, lack of intuition, inability to cover big complexities, its struggle with emotional or fluid realities, inadequacy for private, relationship, creative, and spiritual goals...and its **unattractiveness to more creative brain types.** Plus: **Linear planning, like that of an engineer, often can't satisfyingly capture the desires, visions, and dreams of us women!** While men may need just one calendar for their professional life, most women are juggling multiple for their different roles in life: one for their career, one for family activities, one for the children's sports and school events, one for their volunteer project...

Progress and evolution happen in a fascinating pendulum movement between extremes, although while a normal pendulum stays static and is fixated at an overhead support point, in history or evolution, the swinging from one extreme to the other moves the pivot point upward to higher levels of progress and consciousness.

The same happened with planning styles, too! After the pendulum of history was for a long time on the side of linear, muscular, numerically measurable plans, women and creative, intuitive people were searching for different approaches to planning their work and life! So the pendulum of planning swung to the opposite extreme: the epoche of enlightenment, mysticism, New Age, and, later, the Law of Attraction added a completely new worldview to planning! Suddenly, feelings, intuition, spirits, angels, "downloads" from the "upstairs team," muse's whispers, the power of belief, faith, vision boards, dream catchers, crystals, incense, oracle cards, and pendulums as planning tools were in vogue.

In contrast to the engineer archetype, a new archetype for planning was born, personified by Walt Disney's wonderful figure, **Tinkerbell**!

The Tinkerbell archetype's philosophy of "If you can dream it, you can do it," and quotes like, "Dreams do come true if only we wish hard enough," make her the perfect feminine planner of the mystical realm. The advantages of this planning style are that it has a lot of what the engineer's archetype was missing: It is more fluid and therefore more flexible. It feels more organic, feminine, and fun. Yet, the disadvantages are that it is hard to communicate, repeat, teach, and scale. For groups, teams, or whole corporations it is therefore nearly impossible to use. **That's why Tinkerbell-style planning exists mainly in the realm of personal visions and dreams.**

Evolution progresses by utilizing the best of the previous stages! What archetype integrates and uses the best aspects of the engineer and can combine them with the magical powers of Tinkerbell? **The archetype of the artist!** An artist combines craft, learned technique, and linear tools with guidance from the muse, creative flow, and embrace of the chaotic, mysterious, and unknown. An artist is an engineer with glittering rainbow fairy wings!

The artist's approach is the way I plan. I see my **business and personal life not as separated but rather as connected and interwoven** like the cotton thread of a canvas, and my whole life as my biggest painting. Planning for me is a dance between my heart's vision, defined by my values, strategically mapped by my mind and intuitively executed by my body with presencing and in flow. The two most important keys for successfully planning like an artist are intention and faith in the flow of one's creativity.

Let me share examples of how that looks practically and what becomes possible by living the Intentional Creativity® artist lifestyle. To be crystal clear: I don't mean you have to become a professional painter or artist of any other discipline! It is about using your power of intention and access to your effervescent creativity as a daily way of living.

Mind or Magic?

An old, wise grandmother is teaching her granddaughter about life.
"A fight is going on inside me," she said to the girl. "It is a terrible fight and it is between two wolves. One is evil - he is anger, envy, sorrow, regret, greed, arrogance, self-pity, guilt, resentment, inferiority, lies, false pride, superiority. His name is 'ego.'

She continued, "The other is good - he is joy, peace, love, hope, serenity, humility, kindness, benevolence, empathy, generosity, truth, compassion, and faith. His name is 'soul.'
The same fight is going on inside you - and inside every other person, too."

The granddaughter thought about it for a minute and then asked her grandmother,
"Which wolf will win?"

Her grandmother simply replied, "The one you feed."

As a child inspired by my favorite book, *The Little Witch* by Otfried Preussler, which my mom read to me many times over in bed at night, I deeply believed in the existence of magic. My early childhood answer when adults asked, "What do you want to be when you grow up?" was always enthusiastic: "A witch!" I had little notebooks I doodled and scribbled in before I could write. They were my magic books. Later, my written words were my spells. Spelling and wishing with fervor was my form of planning at that stage!

Sadly, some big disappointments and heartbreak in my late teens and early twenties seeded doubt in my mind about "magic powers." I entered the internal, commonly shared human battle with the two wolves quoted above. For more than 10 years, **I searched for a sense of certainty, control, and safety through academic knowledge** and started to arrogantly look down on anything "mystical," "spiritual," and "new age-y."

Yet it was heartbreak again - two engagements that didn't work out, to be precise - that in my early thirties brought me back into the realm of spirituality, and of my soul. Through what is called the "Avatar Initiation," I experienced for the first time consciously **how it feels to exist as a vast awareness in unity with everything that exists.** It was a life-altering experience. It stopped for a while my inner war of the wolves, the fight between my ego's doubting voice and my muse's whispers. I accepted it as an intuitive knowing and not just as an intellectual concept:

> *"We are not human beings having a spiritual experience;*
> *we are spiritual beings having a human experience."*

> ~ Pierre Teilhard de Chardin

From then on I knew:

1. Magic - as in occurrences unexplainable by sciences - is part of our reality and not just childish imagination.

2. Planning starts with knowing what I am and always getting back to that knowing as a felt embodied experience.

Being 100% aligned with "what I am" is the foundation of any plan of action for creating my desired results.

In the past 25 years, I've had many experiences that defy what science can explain yet which were crucial for me evolving into the woman I am today, able to intentionally create a life I love. I call those my "magic moments." I'll share a few here with the hope that they trigger memories and recognition in you that you have experienced this kind of magic, too!

For example, during a rebirthing self-development weekend retreat in my mid-twenties, I relived my own birth on an energetic level, with visions of extraterrestrial realms in which I was a soul speaking with a divine power about **my choice to incarnate and that I chose a specific couple to be my parents.** The peace that this experience brought me regarding accepting and loving my "flawed parents" is indescribable.

When I was in an unhappy, suffocating career, I was in the bathroom one morning when I saw **my future self, 30 years later, with a haunted, bitter face looking back at me out of the bathroom mirror!** That triggered a sobbing breakdown on the tiled bathroom floor as I realized what staying in that job would cost me. I went to work quitting the job that everyone I knew envied me for. I never regretted that decision!

When I had known Peter for just 48 hours, he held me in an embrace that triggered my earliest conscious memory of when I was two years old: my father carrying me in his arms into our new family home. That memory, combined with nudges from my body, gave me the clear knowing that **this man that I hardly knew was "the one."** Less than seven weeks later he proposed, and we got married the same year.

When we lived in Michigan and were looking online into the real estate market offerings in Southern California, I saw a helicopter shot of a property in a town outside of our search area. The image was blurry and I had no other information about the house. Yet my **"inner compass"** - the same feeling I had when knowing that Peter was my soulmate - told me: "This is it!" And, indeed, we ended up buying the house and live in it now, happily updating it for over 10 years!

Inner Compass Confidence™
The practical steps to creating a life you love

"When we remember what we are and where we came from, planning a life we love becomes as natural as breathing in and out."

~ Sylvia Becker-Hill

Many people, friends, and clients ask me all the time: "How did you become so successful?" "How do you manage to be happy or at least so positive all the time?" "Where do you get so much energy?" "How do you come up with so many creative ideas?"

Here are the steps you can take to answer those questions for yourself:

Step 1: Discover your spiritual answer to the question, "What am I?"

In my experience, the answer reveals itself in stages and changes over the years. My current answer is "loving consciousness."

Step 2: Learn to distinguish if you are living from that embodied knowing of what you truly are or if you are coming from your human ego.

What helps you to distinguish those two ways of operating are your feelings. If you feel expanded, connected, and safe, you are in alignment with your true nature. When you feel tight, disconnected, and stressed, you are coming from your ego being triggered.

Step 3: Develop your visions and goals in moments of connection with your true self and feel for the vision more than you analytically construct it.

Our desires and dreams come from our hearts! Our mind is brilliant for supporting the execution of action steps later. Yet the inception of our "true north" always comes from love!

Step 4: Train your interoception so you can decipher your body's messages.

Interoception is your ability to focus your attention inward into your body and become aware of physical sensations. These can be strong and obvious like a headache or hunger in your belly, or very subtle and nuanced like gentle nudges to go toward or stay away from something.

It was deeply empowering and life-altering when I - a classic, mind-glorifying bookworm - discovered **the neglected super partner in planning and creating my life: my beloved body!** It took me a lot of compassion and forgiveness work to embrace the fact that I abused my body over decades by taking it for granted and not understanding its wisdom to signal to me my level of alignment or misalignment with my values and truth.

Step 5: Follow confidently and intentionally your inner compass through action

By staying conscious of your true nature and learning to use your body's signals as your inner guiding compass, you can drop your old habit of external orientation and come home within yourself.

Yes, we are social beings. Yes, we need others. Yes, we are healthier and live longer in a community of people we can trust and have fun with. BUT!

You don't need anyone to tell you what you want, what is important for you, what to focus on, and what to do next. Your soul, intuition, higher self, or inner muse - whatever you like to call your spiritual self - always knows!

You can calibrate your inner compass consciously through small, simple, daily exercises:

My Inner Compass Calibration Techniques

- **"Ego soothing"** through nervous system regulation by gentle deep breathing and gentle slow rubbing of your fingertips against each other.
- **"Grounding"** through standing with your feet hip-width apart, imagining roots growing deep into the Earth.
- **"Channeling"** – keep a diary and pen beside your bed at all times. Meditate in bed until you are teetering between wakefulness and sleep. Give your subconscious mind a task, a problem to solve, a specific question. Expect to wake up with a download ready for you to capture through fast handwriting into your journal before you do anything else!
- **"Muscle-Testing"** – using your thumb and index finger, make a ring by touching your fingertips together and trying to break that ring with the index finger of your other hand. This way, you can get answers from your body.
- **"Body Pendulum"** – using your standing body's gentle swaying forward or back as a powerful way to get answers from your body.
- **"Dowsing"** using a pendulum on a chain held by your hand to receive answers like yes, no, maybe, wrong question.

Why it Matters That You Plan a Life You Love

"When we think of ourselves as an artist, then every day emerges as a
gorgeous canvas calling us to leave our colors and brush marks on it.
And when we die one day,
we will leave an incredible masterpiece behind.

Yet instead of attracting dust in an attic or
being stored away in a museum,
as businesswomen, we will have touched more lives than we could count
with its beauty."

~ Sylvia Becker-Hill

When you plan and then experience living a life you love, the chances that you are a happy, positive, and kind person are much higher than if you don't! I believe that "happy leaders are better leaders." Happy people love life, other people, and nature, and with that, they protect, care for, and nurture themselves, others, and our environment.

I truly believe that your happiness is your biggest gift to the world!

So go, beloved courageous woman!

Remember what you are: a child of the universe made of love and light.

Say "no" to external shoulds and pressures to behave and act a certain way!

Focus on your intentions and access your creativity to bring them to life.

Strengthen your Inner Compass Confidence™ and follow "your own nose," as we say in Germany. You have everything you need to plan and live a life you love.

Please reach out and tell me how it is going or if I can be of service with some pixie dust!

xoxo,

Sylvia

Prudence Hatchett

PH Counseling, LLC & Learn with Prudence
Mental Wellness Specialist

www.facebook.com/phcounselingllc
www.instagram.com/prudencehatchett
www.phcounseling.orglearn-with-prudence.myshopify.com

Prudence Hatchett is a best-selling author, business owner, licensed counselor, board certified coach, multi-endorsement educator, and multi-certified mental health professional. Prudence Hatchett earned a BA in Psychology and an M.S. in Special Education from Mississippi State University. She earned an M.Ed. in Counselor Education from the University of Mississippi. She owns a private practice, PH Counseling, LLC and ecommerce store and brand, Learn with Prudence. She has over 17 years of combined experience in the mental health and educational fields. She supports people in maturing their mental health and emotional wellness through the power of education, strength exploration, skill building, and elevating confidence.

THE JOURNEY TO DISCOVERING THE LIFE YOU LOVE

By Prudence Hatchett

The mere thought of planning your life for a specific outcome can be daunting. Attempting to be strategic with brainstorming ideas or wrestling with your inner conflicts is enough to send shockwaves through the spine. Effective planning takes intentionality, purposeful action, and self-determination. Before I became enlightened to the fact that I was in control of my own fate, I left too many things to chance. Meaning, I was not an active contributor in my own life, but rather a passive participant. Things started to shift when I became self-aware of my own power to remove obstacles, learn new skills, and walk in my own truth. This was just the beginning of how I formulated a plan to live the life I love.

Love can be a difficult subject to tackle, mainly due to the intricacies of its nature. Even in its purest form, love is a strong emotion to try to capture in one sentence. Think about it. When you say you love something or someone, it is all-consuming. Love is the air you breathe and the water you drink. Love is the kindness we witness in humanity and in the beautiful stillness in the stars. But what happens to the feeling of love when we experience heartache and pain? Well, it starts to disintegrate into small pieces of matter, dissolving into a trail of disappointment.

We are living in a time in which life can be really busy, and several factors are vying for your attention. These factors can cause distractions and interfere with you focusing on your goals. Before you know it, the busyness of life, mundane routines, and consistent responsibilities can lead to a stale life—a life filled with unsatisfactory relationships, multiple health problems, and an insurmountable amount of stress. All of these things together create a place where dreams and aspirations go to die.

Eventually you start to notice that you've been asleep for far too long. Something is starting to boil and stir within you that can no longer be denied. It has been brewing for some time now, and you have probably tried to suppress it. It has felt both heavy and empty at the same time because you can't quite put your finger on it. This feeling is hard to describe because it's stubborn and it will not go away. It demands your attention and it will no longer be denied. If you are reading this book, it means that thing or feeling that has been suppressed is starting to awaken. It is time for you to be happy and authentic. It is time for you to live out loud and on purpose.

I know what you are thinking: "Well, Prudence, that is easier said than done."

And I will respond with, "You are right."

That is a true statement, because, in essence, everything is easier said than done. But that doesn't mean it can't be done or shouldn't be done just because it seems hard. In life, sometimes you will need to think a little harder and sacrifice a little longer. With advancements in technology and knowledge of the inner workings of life, we can eventually conclude we want things to be completed quickly. We want what we want, and we want it now.

If something takes too long to be completed in our imaginary allotted time, then some may be tempted to give up. They drop the ball on their own goals because it is not happening quickly enough. I do not buy into this philosophy. Please go ahead and retire the thought that you have to rush yourself or be in a hurry to get things done. All this serves to do is increase the feeling of anxiety. When anxiety goes up, productivity goes down. This is the opposite of what you want.

Fundamentally, what you want to do is light a match so your productivity can spread like wildfire.

Productivity and Self-awareness

When you are planning a life you love, you will need to create a mental space for productivity to be enhanced. You need a mental space to hear yourself, your authentic self. One of the main ingredients of creating your mental space is self-awareness. Self-awareness is so much bigger than identifying what's on the surface layer of your life. It includes paying attention to your current state of being in multiple areas of your life. Oftentimes, this stage can be skipped because the eye is too focused on the prize or the end goal. Yes, you need the end goal in your sights to build your short- and long-term goals. But it is imperative that you are aware of your starting place and baseline. This is important because you need to take a self-inventory of your existing skill set and the areas you need to improve. Not just any areas of improvement—the specific skills that you are lacking that are needed for your goals. Your time is valuable and you should use it wisely. So why not use it on things that will make you more productive?

To identify your current skillset, I encourage you to think about those things that you do naturally. These are the skills that seem easy to you but may be more difficult for other people to carry out. Think about your hobbies and interests. What are you drawn to when you are not working? What do you do in your spare time? Consider the compliments that you receive from others, no matter how big or small, even if you think some of them are trivial. If you feel comfortable enough, you may even ask some of your closest confidants what they think your skills are, or ask them about your strengths. Think about your classes in school, and identify your highest-graded subjects and extracurricular activities. It is a good idea to create the largest list that you can produce.

Remember, this list is for your awareness. I urge you not to make this list about judging yourself or self-criticizing. Unfortunately, self-judgment comes way too easily for some people. When planning the life you love, you must be aware of your skills and strengths that already exist. This is not the time to be bashful or shy about what you can do or what you can bring to the table. If self-criticism does rear its ugly head, I want you to let those thoughts come and go. Allow them to roll away as if they were being carried in the wind blowing on top of the ocean. Do not allow those thoughts to stick around. If you recognize the negative thoughts repeating, you can implement a countering technique against those thoughts. For example, if you are thinking, "There is no way I am confident enough to sing on stage. Why did I agree to the performance?" you will intentionally counter the thought and say the truth: "I can sing and I feel good when I am singing. I deserve to be heard." The counter-statement must be true and accurate to feel "real." It must be reinforced, meaning it must be repetitive just like the negative thoughts. You can make it easier on yourself by creating a visual cue, such as a post-it on your computer, and reading the counter-statement as if it were an affirmation.

Understanding Weaknesses

Since I have discussed the importance of recognizing your strengths and skillsets, I must also discuss the importance of recognizing your weaknesses. I want to stress the fact that recognizing weaknesses is not the same thing as self-criticism or self-judgment. In fact, understanding your weaknesses is actually a strength, because it means you are self-aware of what you can and can not do. Sometimes people can get carried away with their weaknesses, meaning they tend to list everything they can think of that they don't like about themselves. Unfortunately, then it turns into self-criticism. I always interrupt a client from doing this because I use a strength-based approach when I am working with people. Leading with strengths and working from a place of skills helps to reinforce personal confidence.

How do I use weakness as a strength? Anytime a person is self-aware of their truths, that is always a strength. With keeping the goal of being productive in mind, the weaknesses identified will be related to the skillsets that are making it harder for you to be productive. These missing skills are causing a disruption to productivity or to you completing your goals. You do not need to create a laundry list of weaknesses, nor all the things that you feel may be wrong with you. That is counterproductive to the goal. For example, I don't know how to sing opera, dance ballet, or build houses. But guess what, who cares, because these are not needed for my career or personal life. But if I didn't know how to send an email or work my voicemail, then these behaviors would be considered weaknesses, because I do need to know how to operate them for my business.

Honestly, you don't have to have your goals solidified for you to have a sense that you are lacking certain skills. You already have some idea about what you want your goals to be, even before they are formally written down. For example, you may have dreams of owning a brick-and-mortar bakery but lack skills in understanding lease agreements. I've seen far too many people start something before they do their research and due diligence. Again, this is why self-awareness is very important for both your strengths and weaknesses. And once you figure out what is lacking, you get to learn about it. That's what information literacy is all about—the ability to find, evaluate, organize, use, and communicate information in all its various formats.

The most common ways to learn include reading books, taking courses, attending workshops, and finding a mentor. Planning a life you love will take some form of investment in yourself, such as investing your time and money. Be willing to make financial investments for your own education. Any form of education will always have value and it will serve its purpose. Take the time you need to learn and adjust to new skills.

The Miracle Question

What is the miracle question all about? The miracle question is actually derived from an evidence-based counseling theory. It examines your life without problems present so you can create your dream scenario. This is a thinking question. Resist the urge to answer with "I don't know." In fact, that is not an answer at all. It's an escape strategy. Allowing yourself to think about your life is an intention strategy. So, what is the miracle question?

"If a miracle occurred while you were asleep tonight, what changes would you notice in your life tomorrow?"

I want you to answer the following questions, solely based on your answer to the miracle question:

1. Where are you?
2. Who do you see?
3. What do you see?
4. What foods are you eating?
5. What do you smell?
6. Describe the weather.
7. Are you using any technology?
8. Describe how you look.
9. Are you by the ocean?
10. Do you hear music?

Now, I want you to compare and contrast the similarities between your current life and your miracle life. Describe what is similar and what is different. Does your miracle life include some people, places, or things that are already present in your current life? There is no right or wrong answer, we are only examining thoughts.

Figuring Out What You Love

People can live in a state of survival or the world of "just enough" for far too long. Let me say, I totally understand that hard times can approach us all, and none of us is exempt from bad luck. In the context of planning a life you love, survival mode can overshadow dreams and dampen the spirit. When this happens, it will hinder or completely stop the planning process. So, why did I bring this up? Unfortunately, for various reasons, I see this state of being far too often in people. It is important for me to tell you that it's ok to start dreaming and planning again. Start visualizing and allow your internal spirit to become alive as if it were sprinkled with magical fairy dust.

Start by asking yourself some important questions. Ask yourself, what do you want out of life? Give yourself permission to allow your mind to wander, drift, and dream. Giving yourself permission may sound easy to do, or even redundant at times. But if you have been conditioned to live according to certain stereotypes or you have created a false belief system based on others' negative opinions or negative environmental factors, giving yourself permission is not so easy.

Honestly, we all have some type of conditioning because essentially, that is what behavior is. Behavior conditioning can be either a positive or a negative experience. Either way, we must give ourselves permission. If you have a negative conditioning experience, such as the development of a false belief system, this is likely standing in the way of the life you love. Negative experiences and negative thoughts can prolong the process of giving yourself permission because it could leave you feeling unworthy of such good things. You will need to break down those negative walls and barriers so you can rediscover your authentic self and start to believe again.

Honestly, being asked what you want is a loaded question. This is why giving yourself permission is important—it opens up the mental space for you to think and dream. To help with identifying more of what you want, ask yourself the following questions. Think of these as journal prompts that will help you unlock or rediscover what you want. It is a good idea to write down the questions and your answers. You do not have to add mental tension by trying to remember the questions or memorize your answers. Answer these without self-judgment or criticism:

1. What do you want?
   a. In life?
   b. In religion or spirituality?
   c. In finances?
   d. In friendships?
   e. In your family?
   f. In your romantic relationship?
2. Who and what are the people, places, or things you love?
3. When you think of the word "love," what immediately comes to mind?
4. Can you recite 10 things you love in 30 seconds? Describe them.
5. Who or what are the people, places, or things you loathe?
6. Describe five great experiences that have occurred in your life within the past year.
7. Describe four negative experiences that have occurred within the last two years.
8. Do you have a secret talent that no one else knows about? Describe it.
9. What do you wish you could do better?
10. When considering a life you love, on a scale of 1-10, where would you rate your life now?
    a. What is your reasoning for that rating?
    b. What stopped your rating from being a number lower?
    c. What would it take for your rating to be a number higher?

Please take your time to answer the questions. No need to be in a hurry or rush; that only increases anxiety. To plan a life you love, you must actually know the people, places, and things you love. This type of life does not happen by chance, it happens with intention. It happens on purpose. You need to self-reflect so you can identify what you love and weed out what you don't love. You also need to know the habits and behaviors that no longer serve you. This is a process, not something you get to think about one time. This is your life, you are taking an inventory, and it takes time to process. Keep in mind that you are still in the stage of self-awareness. Remember, self-awareness goes deeper than the surface level.

There are so many instances when I ask clients these or similar questions and they say, "I don't know." A big reason for this is they haven't given themselves enough time to think. Some of us live life on autopilot, and it doesn't take much thought to get through the day, just learned routines. But when asked questions that deviate from their daily thinking patterns, clients often feel stuck. Allow these questions to help you become unstuck and create a new thinking path forward so you can plan the life you love.

Goal Setting and Prioritizing

So far, I have encouraged you to focus on the thinking process and mental exercises. Now, let's focus on goal setting and prioritizing. It's a good idea for goals to be completed in small actionable steps or increments. The rationale behind this is for you to refrain from becoming overwhelmed and stressed on this journey—that is the opposite of planning a life you love. Throughout the thinking process, you probably have started to gravitate toward some specific goals and ideas for your life, maybe even before reading this chapter. When thinking about your goals, consider these questions:

1. What are your goals for yourself?

2. What do you want to do or accomplish?
3. What part of your life do you want to maintain because you already love this area?
4. What skills are you lacking that you need to improve in order to complete your goals?
5. Are you willing to improve those skills?

Then ask yourself:

1. Are your goals doable and realistic?
2. How do you need to prioritize your goals (i.e. complete the easiest step first or the more difficult step first)?
3. Are the steps written in a way that can be completed in small increments?
4. Are the things you love actually included in your goals?

These are questions and answers that should not just be stationed in your head. I encourage you to write them down so you can have a focal point and visual cue. If you try to remember everything too quickly, it likely will only be stored in your short-term memory. If you are not repeating the goals and steps to help you remember (i.e. reinforce), the short-term memory information will not transfer to the long-term memory bank. Instead, you will likely forget it. When we forget things, it's like starting back over at ground zero, never moving toward the implementation phase. Plus, writing things down is a learning tool that will positively reinforce your thoughts (i.e. help you remember it and pass it to the long-term memory).

Hire a Professional

When needed, hire a professional. There are people who are professionally trained to help you along your journey. Yes, a lot of information is free, but the interpretation of how to use it is not. I encourage you to invest in yourself with your time and money. There is a wide range of professional services available to you with just a click on your keyboard. You can even hire service professionals, such as a cleaning service, that could help you free up more of your time. Financially, you may not be able to hire every professional that you need at the same time, but this is where prioritizing and creating small steps can be of good use.

The Journey, Not the Destination

For me, planning the life you love is not about a specific destination, it's about the journey of living your life. Yes, we want to be able to check off our goals and feel a sense of accomplishment. But what happens after those goals are complete? Well, you can start to work on consistency or create new goals; either way, you can learn to love the journey. You can actually enjoy your life while you continue to self-improve. Life happens on a continual basis, and thank goodness it does! It is wonderful to know that we are capable of creativity and we can bring things to fruition. We can help one another live better and be stronger. None of us are meant to live this life alone or be in solitude. We were designed to give and to receive love, not just one time or a specific time, but along the journey.

Creating Your Own Zone

Get enthusiastic about the direction of your life. Create a place that is for you, by you. To create your own special zone, use tools like vision boards and visualizations. Make a vision board by putting together pictures and quotes that represent your dreams and goals. Put it somewhere you can see it every day. Also, imagine yourself achieving your goals regularly. Doing these things helps you build a mental and physical space that matches what you want in life. This special zone becomes a place where your dreams feel real in your mind, inspiring and guiding you toward making them come true in real life. Think manifestation or the law of attraction!

Mental Health

Understanding and prioritizing mental health is crucial to planning the life you love. Our mental well-being significantly influences how we set and pursue goals, make decisions, and navigate life's challenges. When our minds are in a positive state, it becomes easier to envision a fulfilling future and take the necessary steps to achieve it. On the contrary, struggling with mental health issues can impede clarity, motivation, and overall life satisfaction. Taking care of our mental health through self-care, seeking support when needed, and fostering a positive mindset can lay a strong foundation for planning and living a life that aligns with our deepest desires. In essence, a healthy mind is a powerful tool for shaping the life we truly want. Sometimes, not only can life be hard to navigate, but our mental health needs can get confusing. Incorporating the help of a counselor or coach can really be beneficial in building skills and mental resilience.

Embrace Yourself

Do you know that you are the key ingredient in your own life? Self-acceptance is a huge factor when it comes to embracing yourself and generating self-love. So many things can happen in life that overshadow the positive light that you were meant to bring to the world. It's not your fault, nor is it fair to you. Oftentimes, we have to give ourselves what we wish we could have received from other people. We have to understand what hurt us so we can heal ourselves the right way. I'm not talking about just placing a bandaid over the wound (i.e. a quick fix). I'm referring to your soul being healed so you can live in mental freedom and feel accepted. This is also why self-awareness is so important. You must be able to identify self-defeating thought patterns that are keeping you hostage to your own pain. Break free so you can embrace all of who you are, and plan a life you love.

You are more than worthy of having what you want in life. You just have to do one simple thing: believe it. If you don't believe it, ask yourself why. What or who is standing in your way? Get rid of those barriers so you can see yourself clearly. Don't invalidate your beliefs or your feelings. Living authentically means being true to yourself. It's about knowing and accepting who you are without worrying about what others think. To do this, you need to understand your strengths, weaknesses, passions, and quirks, and embrace them. It also involves saying no when needed and setting boundaries to protect yourself. By being honest with yourself and living authentically, you can create a life that makes you happy and peaceful. You get to create the life that you love.

Planning a life you love is no easy feat,
It will take courage and determination,
And even daring imagination.

It will take loving kindness toward the self,
And dreams dusted off the mental shelf.

It will take patience and grit,
As well as the determination not to quit

Planning a life you love is no easy feat,
But unfulfilled potential is deceit.

So find your mark and get ready to start
Count to 10,
and just listen to your heart

-Prudence

Sheree Wertz

DentalHygiene411

Mom, Oral Health Coach, Myofunctional Therapist Author Speaker

https://www.linkedin.com/in/sheree-wertz-43b71a46/
https://www.facebook.com/groups/healthymouthmoms
https://www.instagram.com/dental_hygiene_411/
https://shereewertz.com
https://dentalhygiene411.com

Sheree Wertz is a dedicated mom, dental hygienist and myofunctional therapist with a passion for empowering families to take control of their health and wellbeing. With years of experience in the dental field, Sheree has developed a deep understanding of the critical role oral health plays in overall wellness. Her journey led her to specialize in myofunctional therapy, a niche that allows her to address issues related to breathing, sleep, and oral function.

Everyone has the potential to live their best life and thrive by taking ownership of their health. Sheree's work involves making a difference in people's lives through improved health and increased awareness, empowering families to take action and tweak habits that impact their daily life. Her personalized care and dedication make her a standout in her field, inspiring her families to embrace a healthier, more vibrant lifestyle with her SHIFT method.

YOU'RE THE OWNER
NOURISHING YOUR BODY WITH OXYGEN, WATER, NUTRITION, SLEEP, AND RESPECT

By Sheree Wertz

"Whether you think you can or you think you can't, you're right!"
—Henry Ford

"What we think, we become!"
—Buddha

Look at your current life. Do you have the life you want? If the answer is no...you have the power to create the life you want. It's never too late. Life is a journey; you take it one step at a time, and if you don't like the road you're on, you can always go down another one.

We have been taught that happiness comes from achieving goals or possessing things. In my early 20s, I knew what I wanted for my life and could see it so clearly. I wanted the American dream that everyone wants and is working toward. I decided to be a dental hygienist, get married, have a family, and make a difference in the world. I actually felt the joy of creating the life that I pictured. I could feel it; I knew it was going to happen.

I had almost everything I envisioned by the time I was 25—a husband I loved, who was also my best friend, a successful business that we were building together, and a great work-life balance.

I was happy, but then I found myself asking, "Is this all there is?" We had reached our goals together. Now what? I did not like admitting to myself that I wanted more, and even felt ashamed for thinking that there had to be more to life. I had everything I'd imagined, with the exception of a baby. This is where our next journey/struggle began. We had difficulty conceiving a child.

I can confidently tell you that I knew without a shadow of a doubt that I was going to successfully carry and deliver a baby. It wasn't a wish or a dream; it was an affirmation, a given, a definitive in my mind.

Then we were told by five specialists that what I wanted was not possible; I would never carry a baby to term. We were both devastated. I wish I had the words to explain how I felt each time I was told it was an impossible dream. I believed it was possible. Each time I simply said, "You aren't the right person to help me, so I am moving on until I find that person."

Doctors only know what they are taught, and they treat symptoms—most do not look at the body as a whole. Our body is amazing. There are 11 major organ systems in the body, all working together simultaneously, yet we treat them separately. Our mouth even has its own insurance. Healthcare has become a big business of protocols and pills. Finding help when your problem is outside of what is mainstream can be difficult, yet it is possible.

Determined to have a baby, I was more than confident that I would prove them wrong. I could feel it in my soul with every part of me and see it in my mind…being pregnant, holding and nursing my baby, and watching my child grow into adulthood. It would take two rounds of failed in vitro and eight miscarriages over thirteen years.

I did find the right doctor, and in one of the most unlikely places. A friend of mine had an uncle who was a chiropractor and also practiced Chinese medicine using herbs and acupuncture. That first day, upon listening to my journey and being amazed at my persistence and confidence that I would have a baby, he gave me what I needed most…HOPE! He asked me to give him three months and, true to his word, within three months I was pregnant. We were ecstatic! At six weeks I started spotting. I was so scared at the ultrasound appointment I heard the heartbeat for the first time. It is a wonderful core memory, and we were blessed with a baby girl of our own. The happiest day of our lives. The only name that was appropriate for her was Faith. I tell her all the time that we had to have faith to have Faith!

With the miscarriages behind us, a new baby daughter, and a thriving business again, we had it all. Thirteen months later, an opportunity presented itself to adopt a baby. Based on all we had been through to have Faith, we jumped at the chance to have another child. It was a girl. It was obviously God's plan for us. We were now a family of four and everything was falling into place. I was 38, and my boxes of the picture-perfect life I imagined were all checked off; I had it all. I felt so complete.

Until an adoption is final, the birth mother has a right to change her mind, and this one did. Three months later, I received an email that she was coming to get the baby and she would arrive the next day to pick her up. There were extenuating circumstances, but we had no warning, no phone call, no discussion; we went from the highest of highs to the lowest of lows. It was utter devastation. The loss of a child, even a child that you didn't give birth to, is a devastating experience. It affected all of us. As for Faith, she had a baby sister one day and the next day she was gone. She did not understand, we did not understand; my husband and I each internalized our feelings.

We decided that I would stay home and take care of Faith. It was an opportunity to enjoy the milestones that so many parents have to miss because of work. We'd tried so long to have her, so I felt I should stay home and enjoy being her mom.

We never talked about the loss of the baby; we moved on like it never happened. It was the beginning of a long journey of loss for our family. Life would never be the same.

In a matter of months, we would lose our baby, our nephew to suicide, our beloved dog, and other family members and friends to illnesses.

There didn't seem to be an end to the loss, and I felt so alone. We could not get back to that feeling of utter bliss.

It was then that I began to question life. How can we have everything we worked years to achieve and still be feeling empty?

What I was to learn was that it wasn't an authentic reflection of who I was or wanted to be. I would finally discover why I wasn't content.

Maslow's Hierarchy of Needs

Maslow's hierarchy of needs states that once your basic needs are met, there is a need for self-actualization and transcendence. He stressed the importance of focusing on the positive qualities of people as opposed to treating them as a bag of symptoms. Maslow argued that the failure to have needs met at various stages of the hierarchy could lead to illness.

Our actions are motivated by certain physiological and psychological needs that progress from basic to complex, explaining human motivation based on the pursuit of different levels of needs. Once our basic needs are met, there is a need to pursue and fulfill one's unique potential.

Self-actualization is the complete realization of one's potential and the full development of one's abilities and appreciation for life. This concept is at the top of Maslow's hierarchy of needs, so not every human being reaches it.

Why is it that very few humans reach this? My theory is that the majority of people are living in fight or flight, just surviving to meet their very basic needs, yet they do not realize it.

According to society, wealth should be our greatest achievement. Houses, cars, status. If you achieve this you will be happy. Right? Not really. We work our whole lives to achieve this dream, only to find out it is not what makes us truly happy.

My husband came home from work one night with a box that contained all of my belongings from the office. He said he no longer needed me there. He had never talked to me that way before. I was stunned, confused, and hurt that he had made a decision without even discussing it with me. We discussed everything. I had no idea what was happening. Where was this coming from? It was a decision he had made and I was supposed to live with it.

A couple of days later, I took my daughter to a birthday party next to our receptionist's house and noticed a for sale sign in her front yard. I asked my husband if he knew why she was moving. He told me it was her story to tell. That didn't make sense to me, but I let it go. A few days after that, I was looking at our cell phone bill and I noticed constant calls between the two of them at all hours of the day and night, including weekends. When I questioned him, he blew me off, saying it was things about the office. He added that during my absence from the office, she had been really helpful to him.

Eventually more and more came out, and we were headed for divorce. In an instant, my life as I knew it would change. This time I would lose my family, my house, my job, and the life we had built.

My world was shattered; it was one of the worst times of my life. I truly did not know what to do. I lost myself. I shut down for a while because it took me time to sort it all out. It certainly was one of the most demoralizing experiences.

It was a painful journey. I had no choice but to deal with it. My idyllic life no longer existed.

For the first time in my life, I didn't know what I was doing or what I wanted. I would spend years replaying how this happened and why. What did I do? What did I not do? How did I get here?

I didn't know who I was or who I was supposed to be now. The biggest takeaway from this situation? It's not about what happens to you; it will always be about what YOU do with what happens to you. It's not the event but the response. My response wasn't the best during this time; I blamed myself, and the most difficult person to forgive is yourself.

We are not taught to love ourselves and put our own needs first. It was not until I was diagnosed with breast cancer during the COVID-19 pandemic that I was forced to look at my life. I believe my inability to stop replaying what had happened in my head created the cancer in my body.

I let my experience and what others thought about me make me feel like I did not know what I was talking about. I gave away my power. I did not follow my instincts, I did not listen to myself. I let the noise drown me out. I did that through how I thought and felt about myself.

There are three things that cause disease: trauma, toxins, and thoughts. Your mind is what sends signals to your body, so if you change your thoughts, you can change biology.

We all have viruses, bacteria, cancer, and parasites in our body, and when our immune system shuts off, they grow. We all already have the disease; they are called opportunistic organisms. We give them the opportunity to cause disease or not.

Western medicine gives you three options to treat cancer: cut it out, burn it out, or poison it and yourself.

I would have to face my fears, and I learned just how much power I have.

> *"F-E-A-R has two meanings:*
> *Forget Everything and Run, or Face Everything and Rise.*
> *The choice is yours."*
> —Zig Ziglar

Cancer opened my eyes. True wealth is health, peace of mind, a life with options, and financial freedom. If you live your life with intention, you don't need a lot of money to have these things. What you do need is to know what that looks like for you, and only you. Prioritize and make a plan.

My cancer brought me full circle to what I know to be true. We really just need a simple life meeting our basics. Being with our family and friends downsizes our lives so we can enjoy it before it's over.

I was lucky my gums started bleeding. That is how I found the cancer. Your mouth is a window into your body and it gives you warning signs.

Although I did not feel this way at first, it ended up being a blessing. What I found was that we create the environment in our body for health or disease. We are told it is our genes that predispose us to illness. However, less than 5 % of the population have illnesses that come from our genes.

Not one person in my family had breast cancer. Most illnesses are epigenetic, meaning they are caused by our environment, our habits, our thoughts, and our beliefs. I shared part of my story because I am positive that my fear, anger, pH, and environment created the cancer in my body.

We can change our genes, our thoughts, and our habits, and create a healthy environment in our mind and body. We have billions of cells in our body that are signaled by our thoughts.

Health has many dimensions and means different things to different people.

If you do not make time for your wellness you will be forced to make time for your illness

These quotes resonate with me because I lived them. Like so many women, I did not make time for myself. I did not put myself first. **Self-**

care is not selfish! We all want to live longer, but many of us have not added that we want to live longer and be healthier.

Lifespan equals the duration of existence in your body. Healthspan measures *healthy* life expectancy. When we talk about creating a life we love, most people will think about wealth. Health is not considered an investment. However, if we do not put our health first, we will spend our wealth getting our health back.

Healthspan is the period of life spent in good health, free from chronic diseases and the challenges of aging. It is not merely the absence of disease, but the state of complete physical, mental, and social well-being. How healthy you will be during your life depends on your mindset. Will you wait to treat the symptoms or start with prevention?

This leads us to conversations about the prevention of age-related diseases and healthy choices.

I got a part-time job working for mobile dentists where we saw kids at school to meet their dental needs. I saw firsthand that cavities are the #1 preventable childhood disease. After everything that happened in my life, I set out to change this statistic. This is what I found on this journey.

The Power of Thoughts and Mindset- Mind-Mouth-Body Connection

Knowledge is a very important tool for positive change. The more knowledge we have, the better choices we can make to live a healthier life. A happy, healthy life starts from the top down with your mind, your thoughts, how you breathe, and respecting the one body you get. You are your greatest asset, your best investment to living your best life.

You are the one and only **OWNER**. You must meet your basic needs in order to thrive!

Oxygen—A Life Supporting Gas

We start and end our life with oxygen! Breathing is essential to life. We take our first breath through our nose when we are born and our last one through our mouth when we die.

When we talk about health, how we breathe is where we should start.

Most living things need oxygen to survive. Oxygen helps organisms grow, reproduce, and turn food into energy. Humans get the oxygen they need by breathing through their nose into their lungs. Oxygen gives our cells the ability to break down food in order to get the energy we need to survive.

The brain represents just 2% of a person's body weight, yet it uses about 20% of the body's oxygen supply. Without oxygen, the brain can't perform even the most basic functions. When we mouth-breathe, we get 18% less oxygen to our brains, it dries out our mouths, and is the leading cause of dental disease. If we truly want to be healthy, we need to assess how we are breathing.

Water—More Than Just Hydration

We have always been told to drink eight glasses of water a day, but do you know why?

America is dehydrated, and that's a problem because water makes up 50-70% of your body weight. 83% of your lungs is water, which may actually explain why water is essential for every organ in our body to function properly. Dehydration can cause fatigue, chills, constipation, dizziness, muscle cramps, confusion, headaches, and other health issues.

Water protects the tissues and joints, keeps the body's temperature normal, and helps it to get rid of wastes. It's the fuel for our body and how we are able to detoxify and deliver oxygen and nutrients to our cells while eliminating toxins that would make us sick.

Remember the famous line, "Water, water everywhere and not a drop to drink," in Samuel Taylor Coleridge's poem, "The Rime of the Ancient Mariner." Water is all around us, but is often not clean or safe enough to drink. Water has a neutral pH of 7.0, and the pH balances our body. No disease happens in the body if our pH is in balance.

Clean water is vitally important for survival. But what is the best water to drink? It depends on who you ask.

Nutrition—Fueling the Body

One of the major shifts in modern medicine is recognizing the role of mouth and gut health and the role our food plays. The purpose of food is to provide nourishment for our bodies, as well as enjoyment, bringing people together to share a meal.

I like the term "food as medicine." The fact is that the food we eat either fuels our bodies or creates inflammation. Much of our food these days is processed, creating inflammation in the body, and is actually making us sick.

Our current healthcare system is not focused on disease prevention and providing healthy foods. It is a business, treating symptoms and handing out pills for every ill. This is where food as medicine comes into play.

Our bodies are amazing. If we give it proper nutrition with food it can heal itself. You are what you eat! Food will either create inflammation in the body or heal it. Sugar creates inflammation and it is in most of the food we eat by design when we feed our body sugar it craves more. Making healthy choices by staying on the perimeter of the grocery store while shopping is a good start to creating healthy habits when it comes to food options. Another good rule is if you can grow it it is good for you. Stay away from processed foods as much as possible.

Since the cancer, I have had the opportunity to work with Dr Kelly Shockley, who says, "If you are not testing you are guessing." We do tests to see exactly what my body needs and use nutrition to restore my health.

Enough Sleep—The Underrated Healer

Chronic sleep deprivation is linked to poor physical and mental health, including weight gain, obesity, diabetes, heart disease, weakened immune system, poor growth, anxiety, depression, poor memory, and ADHD symptoms.

Kids grow while they sleep. We store our memories from the day while we sleep. Our bodies and brains "clean up" and detoxify the day's toxic load while we sleep.

Mouth breathing can disrupt the natural sleep cycle, leading to lighter, less restorative sleep, putting our body into fight or flight. This disruption can affect our mood, energy levels, blood pressure, weight, and overall health.

Given the right conditions, our body does heal itself. We heal mostly when we sleep.

You can reprogram your subconscious mind. Everything starts with how you perceive it.

Whatever you want to achieve in life you work out in your sleep. Your subconscious mind is responsible for 95% of your reprogramming. It is harder to change than habits.

We work through repetition. Think about anything you have learned. You don't need to do anything once you do it over and over to learn what you need to know when your subconscious is highly active. Your subconscious helps you find solutions.

You set yourself up for success when you ask your subconscious mind for answers.

As you sleep, your subconscious is wide awake. Think about what you need to do, and ask your subconscious how you can figure out any problems you have.

Health, wealth, and relationships—ask yourself about this as you drift off to sleep. Your subconscious will figure it out. Do this through repetition and the answer will find you.

Respect

At the end of the day, it is you who is ultimately responsible for what happens in your life.

Whatever you believe, you are right! If you believe something is good for you, it will be good. If you believe it is bad, it will be bad. This is how I started this chapter. You get one body. You are the owner and you must meet your basic needs to not only survive but thrive.

It starts with your mindset, how you breathe, what you put in your mouth, how much sleep you get, respecting yourself, and living your life with intention.

What do you want? Go make it happen with your thoughts and your actions.

Integrating Practices into Daily Life

Your perception, your mind, and how you see things control biology. When people say a gene is turned on or turned off, it means the gene is a blueprint. It is not on or off, you are not a victim of your genes. The only thing you are a victim of is your thoughts.

You do get things from your parents that are passed down. But if you change your perception, you change the reading of the genes.

Your body follows your thoughts. The brain interprets the signals and controls behavior and genetics. The function of the brain is perception.

You can change your life at any time by changing your perception.

Have you ever heard of the placebo effect? It works like this: You have a positive thought that something can heal you—even if it is a sugar pill, you believe it is the real medicine. You heal yourself—it is not the pill that heals you, it is the thought that heals you!

Statistics show that one-third of all healing, even surgery, is the placebo effect.

In the same way that positive thinking can heal you, negative thoughts can kill you.

Habits, Identity, Change

Awareness of habits is key to behavior change, as people often lack clarity rather than motivation.

Habit stacking involves creating new connections in the brain to build new habits, and the right trigger can make a big difference in success.

Forming good habits is easier than breaking bad ones, but changing beliefs is the most challenging.

If you're having trouble with changing habits the problem isn't you, the problem is your system. Bad habits repeat themselves not because you don't want to change but because something's wrong with the system that you have created for yourself.

Reshape the way you think and give yourself the tools and techniques you need to transform your habits.

You owe it to yourself to become everything you have ever dreamed of being. You have the power. It may be hard to believe depending on where your mindset is. But it is that easy. If you can imagine it, visualize it, and feel like it is happening now, at this present moment, you can create it. Don't let the negative thoughts in—if they do pop in, say, cancel, cancel, cancel.

They say life is what happens while you are busy making other plans. But in reality, life is what happens when you don't make plans or don't have a vision of what is next. Believe it or not, the universe gives you what you ask for. What you think is powerful, and what you ask for, good or bad, is what you get. That is why whatever you think, you're right.

Through all of this, I pivoted and became an Orofacial Myofunctional Therapist, dedicated to transforming lives by addressing functional concerns related to the muscles of the mouth and face. There are times when we cannot do things on our own. We need support and guidance.

I specialize in providing integrative and holistic myofunctional therapy solutions that bridge the gap between health and harmony within the body. I am passionate about helping individuals unlock their full health potential and live more fulfilling, balanced lives.

When we know better we can do better. Change your habits, change your life.

Stephanie Dauble

The Fullest Stories
Founder and Principal Designer

https://linkedin.com/in/stephaniedauble
https://facebook.com/sdauble
https://www.instagram.com/daubleganger
https://medium.com/@stephanie.daublestephanie.nyc

Stephanie Mary Dauble is an Internationally acclaimed bestselling author, established corporate executive, and accomplished principal designer best known for her passion for reframing the plight of generational addiction and mental illness and inspiring the world to create beauty from broken. She is a tenacious leader whose professional and personal experiences, uncommon perspective, and zeal for life make her well-positioned to untangle complex paradigms that help illustrate all sides of a story with humanity and grace. Stephanie believes navigating our most traumatic experiences with grit and gratitude can lead to extraordinary beauty, unexpected fulfillment, and lasting generational change. Her lifetime body of work is reverently curated, wholeheartedly sincere, and tangibly reflective yet remarkably relatable, thus allowing her audience to feel along with her. Stephanie believes that no matter our origin story, we should always strive for bliss.

THE BLISS MANIFESTO: MAPPING A LIFE OF MEANING AND MAGNIFICENCE

By Stephanie Dauble

Self Help

Introduction
The Divine Art of Life Mapping

"Though no one can go back and make a brand new start, anyone can start from now and make a brand new ending."
—Carl Bard

If you grew up around people who intentionally plan big, you'll know its value. You'll know that creating a map for your one and only extraordinary life is consequential. If you were not around big planners, you might think it's too hard, too time-consuming, or not for you. Perhaps winging it has been your strategy. You may even love the idea of creating a meaningful life map—one that feels juicy, ambitious, challenging, and full of legacy-worthy goals—but you're starting from a place of fear, pain, or overwhelm, and it feels more like a to-do than a ta-da! If any of these things feel remotely true, I invite you to read *The Bliss Manifesto: Mapping a Life of Meaning and Magnificence.* In it, we'll flirt with the idea of why legacy matters, offer a new perspective on why some people get and stay stuck, and explore how writing a few simple sentences from a blissful state can become a north star for stepping into the full spectrum of our greatness.

Chapter 1

A Wish for Better

"What you leave as a legacy is not what is etched in stone monuments, but what is woven into the lives of others."
—Anonymous

Over a delicious limoncello martini with a friend, I shared a few details of a new story I'd been working on. With all the corresponding hand gestures, I excitedly explained my provocation on how the intentionality of a life plan can ensure we don't fall into a deep dark hole of generational trauma caused by the trappings of addiction and how that can translate into leaving behind a meaningful and positive legacy. Phew.

With that, I sat back, tall in my seat, resting my hands gently, proudly, around the long, cold stem of the chilled glass, eagerly awaiting her exuberant embrace of my world-class theme and overall intellectual prowess.

"H'm," she says with a wince. "Sounds morbid."

I've thought about the story I'll leave behind for as long as I can remember. I didn't always know it was called a legacy—the word legacy itself being a newer word in my repertoire within the last fifteen years or so. Still, I've always been curious about what I could do in my lifetime to leave the world better than I found it. Growing up the daughter of a junkie, our world was messy, so leaving the world better seemed like light work. My bar for greatness was set pretty low. I don't recall if my childhood draw to understand significance started with Dad bringing me and my little brother and sisters to church every Wednesday night and twice on Sundays or with Mom bringing us to a drug house on some non-churchgoing days. Perhaps it was partly inspired by the striking dichotomy and life lessons I gleaned from both.

The phrase *leaving a legacy* sounds cliché now, but it wasn't such a commonplace ideology in the '80s before everyone added doing good to their list of must-dos. However, I still imagined that, secretly, most people thought and cared about how other people would remember them after they were gone. Perhaps I was somewhat prematurely nudged into thinking about legacy early on because, over a single decade, I witnessed heroin destroy Mom—and thus, tangentially, our small family—and take with it any hope she had of realizing her dreams. The malevolent agent of addiction wrote her legacy for her.

On the day of Mom's funeral, I was underwhelmed by how few people showed up. There wasn't a choir. No eulogies. No friend groups in corners of the funeral parlor, reminiscing softly, waxing poetically, and remembering that one time when. I suppose it was befitting. It was the kind of empty funeral you might expect for a typical junkie—isolation begets isolation. But I was there, as were my younger siblings, Dad, Grandma, Grandpa, and about a dozen other family members and friends who came out, not because they respected her but because they loved us. And at the moment we paid our final respects, my baby sister got on her tippy toes—her tiny hands wrapped tightly around the cream-colored, crushed poly-rayon fabric that bordered the top of the mid-grade casket as she tried in vain to pull herself up to have a peek before a stranger closed the fancy box and wheeled Mommy off forever. I don't remember who whisked my baby sister from the scene, but I do recall it was a profound moment for me—two people, one at the beginning of her life and one at the end—neither seemingly at peace.

If you ask my now-adult baby sister today, she doesn't remember that moment. She doesn't remember much about Mom at all. But I do; I remember Mom before, during, and after heroin's stronghold created chaos in our lives. I recall the many enchanting days before Mom got sick. I think back to her natural beauty, goofy sense of humor, and intrinsic knack for interior design. And I hark back to almost the precise moment when the storms rolled in, and everything changed. I recall watching ambulances collect her after numerous suicide attempts. I also remember when she finally quit drugs—a few weeks before her death—only to realize that in the fullness of time, it was already too late; her young yet decrepit body was actively shutting down, and the ensuing fatal stroke was, according to her doctors, inevitable. I also think back to people expecting this to be her fate. After all, Mom came from generations of people in pain, many of whom succumbed to the execrable grip of addiction—this became their legacy. And, without the relentless pursuit for a better life, it could be, and statistically speaking should be, my legacy, too, if I let it be. If we care about the story we leave behind, we must write, plan, own, and advocate for it. If we don't take control of every aspect of our narrative, someone else will.

From that moment and countless more, I vowed to do whatever I could to avoid a similar fate. I was aware of the statistics and the unlikelihood that I would ever become much of anything in my lifetime; however, I owed it to myself, my family—both past and present—and my Creator to try. I decided to do my part in shifting our generational paradigm by rewriting a new middle to my family's traumatic yet expected plot——one that's befitting of all the love, joy, and purpose possible in a lifetime. I resolved to give myself the gift of self-love instead of self-loathing, caring instead of carelessness, intentionality instead of indifference, forgiveness instead of fear, and redemption instead of recklessness. Perhaps if I could lean into my family's trauma, learn from it, and embrace the discomfort, I could avoid the blind spots and catastrophic pitfalls of my ancestors. With focused hard work and speculative good fortune on my side, I believed I could create a new legacy for my family and change our trajectory forever.

For these reasons and more, I've always believed that a mission and legacy are the antithesis of morbid. Trying to do one's best in the spirit of leaving the world better than we find it is a noble goal. As the theory of The Butterfly Effect tells us, one small change can affect everything. One article written with love and revelation has the power to change lives. One shame-filled truth shared to help someone else pummels barriers and reminds us that we are worthy and not alone. One brave conversation that confronts and challenges old or biased thinking can help shapeshift dangerous paradigms. One provocation over a delicious limoncello martini can catalyze the plot of meaningful stories that live beyond us. It's all connected. We are all connected. As a single butterfly fluttering upstream causes a downstream tsunami, my small actions may have a lasting impact for good. Every one of us has a connected, universal legacy to create that is far too critical to leave open to chance.

Chapter 2

Which Way is Up?

"Your own self-realization is the greatest service you can render the world."
—Ramana Maharshi

There are countless reasons why ruts materialize in our lives. We may recognize that we deserve more; however, negative self-talk, resulting in a self-imposed spiral, keeps us in the past. I've tried numerous tactics to stay faithful to my calling. I studied the greats, hoping enlightenment would stick. For a time, I thought that creating plentiful to-do lists and working harder than anyone else would lead to lasting fulfillment. And even though my unwavering perseverance and endless planning did help me accomplish what I felt was relative progress, in the depths of my soul, I was convinced that simply by default and proximity, the painful and embarrassing generational social stigmas of my family applied to me too, leading me to retreat from my full potential. My limiting beliefs suppressed my enthusiasm. I took a dozen steps back with every step forward, questioning my worthiness at every turn.

What if anyone found out about my embarrassing family? I couldn't bear the thought of people looking at me the way they used to—all judgy and scared that if they came too close, they'd somehow catch Mom's addiction. I never told anyone I felt this way; I didn't have to. The evidence was in the life I chose to live. Perhaps I was fooling myself into thinking I could rise above generations of pain—anything resembling abundance and freedom felt somewhat disingenuous. Feeling bad didn't feel good. And feeling good didn't feel good, either. At the time, I would describe it as having a faulty compass. At the core, I craved feeling a solid foundation beneath my feet—a grounded place where I could make well-informed decisions.

I yearned to know north. I recognized solid foundations in others and knew it was possible, yet I needed to figure out how to arrive there myself. And then, one day, I learned about a phenomenon that had no apparent correlation to my life yet resonated in a way that felt so deeply personal that I had to explore the connection. It was a high-profile event, and there was no way to avoid the news coverage—a skilled pilot crashed his tiny plane into the ocean only a few miles offshore from Martha's Vineyard. It quickly became evident that although the pilot was technically at fault, due to the night sky and foggy conditions, spatial disorientation was the cause. I was at once saddened by the loss of life and struck by the thought that even with all of his training, hundreds of hours of flight time under his aviator hat, and state-of-the-art dials in the cockpit, he could become so disoriented that he would trade the facts indicated by trusted equipment for a gut feeling. The more I researched this phenomenon at the time, the more I could relate to the disorientation of misplaced trust.

Exploring The Chaotic Weightlessness of Emotional Spatial Disorientation

"To know yourself, you must sacrifice the illusion that you already do."
—Vironika Tugaleva

The grocery shopping takes me about two hours to complete every other week. Somehow, I always pick the cart with the squeaky, wobbly wheel in the front, and even though I know it's a problem right away, I keep the derelict cart while feeling annoyed about it the entire time. I slowly push the giant cart with the squeaky wheel along the long, wide isles of too-tall-for-me-to-reach shelves, with the best stuff seemingly always at the tippy-top while ensuring I'm mindful to check the end dates and cost of everything before adding to the cart. Week after week, the grocery list is mostly the same, with my favorite go-to meal to prepare to be beef stew in the crock pot. I love the crock pot—it's efficient by design, and I play outside with the other kids while dinner is essentially making itself.

For years, before I offered to grocery shop for our family, we had fast food for every dinner; sometimes, it was all we had for weeks, depending on the situation. For some kids, fast food is a treat, but growing up, it was a way of life for us. We craved a home-cooked meal. We longed to have one of those dinners we watched on TV where a family sat together and talked about their day, but there was little chance of that happening anytime soon; it's almost impossible to pin down a junkie on a rampage for a fix.

I can't stand that everything at home feels unconsidered and unhealthy. I want to do my part to infuse order into our house, where the grown-ups are often disorderly and unreasonable. Everything feels upside down, or at least I think it does; I can't tell. Deciphering a healthy emotional attitude feels nearly impossible in the throes of an addict's whims and ensuing co-dependent sustained chaos.

The moments in the tiny plane before the famous crash must have felt like chaos, too.

It's estimated that 90% of pilots who experience spatial disorientation mid flight perish. Spatial disorientation occurs when the pilot can't orient him or herself. It can happen during a dark, starless night, storm, fog, or even simply by losing sight of the horizon. What is up feels down, and what is down feels up. Reality gets flipped. Pilots are trained to use instruments to help them out of this sensory disorder. In times of uncertainty, they typically trust their highly evolved dials to direct them to safety; however, even with state-of-the-art data about their position, some pilots will lose their bearings and trust their distorted reality, ignoring the warnings and ultimately crashing. As the daughter of an addict, I can empathize with how scary it is to have no sense of perspective or direction. The dread of an imminent crash resonates with me. During the decade of our suffering, in the absence of boundaries, a faulty metaphorical control panel, and reversed parent and child roles as a standard operating procedure, I often experienced a sense of chaotic weightlessness, which I describe as lacking a clear emotional horizon.

So, what happens when the grown-ups responsible for equipping their children with a set of dials—tools that help them decipher a metaphorical north—don't exist? An observer might see the grown children of people with addiction as self-saboteurs, people who can't seem to get their act together or help themselves from crashing; however, I believe it's more complex and nuanced. Given that the human brain relies on habits, rituals, and pattern recognition to survive, if a horizon isn't set, a person may experience emotional spatial disorientation for part or all of their life until they or someone else interrupts the pattern and resets the coordinates.

We've all experienced some version of this in our lives to varying degrees: a stormy relationship, uncertainty at a crossroads, a traumatic event that unexpectedly throws our life off kilter. We could be making decisions from a place of fear, thus ignoring the emotional controls that direct us toward clarity and safety. Until I connected the dots of the disorienting realities of navigating life without a clear horizon, I blamed myself for not being strong or resilient enough. Only after I realized that if trained professionals with the proper skills and equipment can lose their way, then children raised with minimal life guidance need more than a wing and a prayer to ensure basics like mental and physical well-being are instilled, not to mention the up-leveling required for more. It is worth taking the time to heal and level out our horizon. After all, legacy hangs in the balance.

Living our most meaningful life—the one that cannot be replicated by another human being now or ever—is not linear, but it's also not complicated. Clues to our greatness can hide in plain sight in the things we're naturally good at and love to do. Our five-year-old self could teach us oodles. Our life's path is deeply personal, resoundingly unique, and apparent if we allow intentional stillness in moments of uncertainty and listen to our divinely-led inner knowing.

Chapter 3

The Bliss Manifesto Explained

"Use me, God. Show me how to take who I am, who I want to be, and what I can do and use it for a purpose greater than myself."
—Martin Luther King Jr.

We have approximately 67,000 thoughts each day. Most of those thoughts are subconscious, meaning most of what we think and do happens on autopilot. For example, have you ever driven to your parents' house, work, or the store, or been on public transit and realized you were at your destination without thinking about how you got there? That is our subconscious in action. It works for us and can work against us, too, in that life can pass us by in the blink of an eye. Everyone talks about how the years seem to accelerate as we get older. Of course, they do. The more things we do on autopilot or via the subconscious, the less opportunity we give our minds to break an old pattern and change our future trajectory. It's one of the reasons some of the world's most successful contributors get up before dawn, read something new, jump into freezing pools, break a sweat, travel, and more—every single day. All these things interrupt patterns, engage our senses, and force us to be present in the moment. Top global contributors also don't leave their minutes, days, weeks, years, and legacy to chance—they have a plan. Almost without exception, they've done deep work to define their why. They have a vision, a mission, and detailed short-term and long-term next steps that outline the various paths to their dreams, sometimes down the minute. They are relentless about advocating for their best life. After achieving some personal and professional success, most world-class contributors far exceed their original plan and, therefore, are constantly reinventing their plan—continually pummeling their limiting beliefs. They've essentially mastered the art and science of pattern-breaking, thus allowing divine energy to take hold of their dreams. Once open and away from the stronghold of the subconscious, they become moldable vessels for flow and the manifestations of divinity through their contributions.

I wanted to be a moldable vessel for flow and abundance, too. But when I tried to dream a bigger dream, plan to the minute, or take a cold plunge like the gurus, I would shortly after revert to the comforting discomfort of my subconscious—the reverse polarity of my faulty compass, confusing the old lies of my family's generational paradigms with the divine truths of love, light, and purpose.

But then, one day, I experienced a divine moment of truth and clarity that changed my life forever. I was in South Laguna Beach, where the sea level dramatically shifts within a few miles of itself, and the Pacific

Ocean crashes against jagged, earth-colored cliffs. The setting sun was orange and heavy, gently falling into the sea as the last pleasant kisses of daylight frolicked across my skin. Warmth radiated through every fiber of my being. I didn't know my lungs could breathe such deep, revitalizing breaths. I felt connected to my surroundings and God like never before. At that moment, my old narrative vanished; my horizon was clear and stable, and I could only feel serenity and peace. I felt gratitude for everything—all the good and all the bad in equal measure, as if they were working in unison toward grace and mission. I thought to myself, if this is bliss, I want more. Ah, yes, *this* is what the gurus are talking about. I want to bottle all this goodness and have access to a bliss genie whenever I'm at a crossroads. Imagine if all life's decisions materialize from this state of pure warmth and gratitude.

At that moment, I made a list of every meaningful thing I would experience if I could co-create it from this state of bliss. What would health, spirituality, family, career, mission, love, and legacy look like in this state? From this position of peace, there is no emotional spatial disorientation. From this place of grace, serving others feels intuitive, divine, and the only way to live. There are no self-saboteurs. Only clarity and connection to what feels right exist.

What bliss feels like to me.

Abundance. The weather is 72 degrees and sunny, with a light northern breeze and low humidity. I live beautifully by the sea in an elegantly designed, beautifully curated home filled with freshly arranged flowers. A south-facing, sun-drenched home with sweeping French doors, left open to the resonating sound of waves crashing. I create experiences that inspire beauty from broken and write many bestselling books, screenplays, and songs from this place that feels more like home than any other home I've ever known. I do significant, meaningful, legacy-worthy work to strengthen humanity. I am surrounded by luxury and savor luxurious experiences with people I treasure. I celebrate relationships that expand my thinking—and theirs—plus spark joy and inspire delight in the people I serve: optimal vitality, financial freedom, and blissful happiness. I am blessed with mutual love, admiration, security, intimacy, and passion with the man God created just for me. I love deeply, live compassionately, and experience joy and gratitude. I live every day full out in the service of others.

No two Bliss Manifestos are the same, like snowflakes and fingerprints—unique and divine. The Bliss Manifesto is a love letter written to and from yourself, capturing your most profound, heartfelt desires in the most significant categories of your life. How do you know if writing your own Bliss Manifesto is meant for you? If you're reading this, it is. Whether you realize it or not, wanting to plan this one extraordinary life is a telltale sign that meaning and legacy are important to you. Perhaps you've never thought you were purpose-driven, or maybe you think about legacy every day. Either way, I believe a Bliss Manifesto in action can help harness our power by keeping us on the right track. We each have a critical role to play that only we can perform. It's worth checking in with ourselves to ensure we're not just settling, biding time until retirement, or waiting for cavalry to arrive. As a boss of mine used to say, the cavalry isn't coming; we are the cavalry. It's easy to get lost, exhausted, or disenchanted with life, and disconnecting and tuning out can be easier. But we are made for more.

The truth is, we are all destined for greatness. Sometimes, greatness manifests in unseen or uncelebrated ways. Sometimes greatness manifests as fame and fortune, but mostly, it does not. It usually shows up in the millions of little things that no one sees that change the world for the better, lest we misinterpret money for meaning and stardom for significance. When I speak of my legacy, it's with the understanding that the tangible impacts will likely be understated in my lifetime, but it doesn't diminish the significance. As I write this chapter, several items on my Bliss Manifesto have come to pass, and some have not yet. In the fullness of time, everything on my manifesto will come to pass—

—as will yours when you write your extraordinary heart-led vision on paper. Of that, I am sure.

We've all got to start somewhere. Whether we're the daughters of junkies or sons of kings, we all have the potential for inimitable greatness; there are no exceptions. Some will employ their greatness for good. Others will weaponize and misuse their talents for evil, and many will squander their gifts or settle for mediocrity. Still, it doesn't change the universal truth that we all possess the potential for magnificence. The Bliss Manifesto is one small step in capturing our essence, including the intrinsic gifts predestined within us, letting those truths help light our path, and, with that goodness as our metaphorical north star, leaving our fine imprint hereafter.

Bethany Klaco

Founder of Free By Design

https://www.facebook.com/iambethanyann
https://www.instagram.com/free.by.design/
https://linktr.ee/free.by.design

Bethany is a Human Design Intuitive Guide and Founder at Free by Design. Her Human Design readings are unique and customized to each individual. She is passionate about empowering women to lead fearless, unapologetic and authentic lives via the power of Human Design. Human Design combines science and spirituality, giving you a unique blueprint for how to best live your life. As a 4/6 Emotional Generator, her superpower is being able to break down complex information systems into bite size, actionable chunks for quick transformation. When you learn your energy type and how to align your actions with your energy, you stress less and life becomes more fun. After your reading with Bethany, you will have unique insight into your energy type and how to best make decisions going forward. It's time to take your power back and plan a life you love!

HUMAN DESIGN: YOUR PERSONALIZED MANUAL FOR LIFE

By Bethany Klaco

Have you ever found yourself wishing there was a manual for your life? A guidebook to lead the way, something to tell you what to do, how to make the best decisions, and what the best path forward for you is? How many times have you found yourself debating a decision, running something over one thousand times in your mind, looking for an answer? Do you know that the average woman spends seven hours a week making decisions?! We waste so much time deliberating. Today, I am here to tell you that there is an easier way forward.

The answer lies in the complex system of Human Design. Human Design is like a modern, upgraded take on astrology. It's the place where science and spirituality meet. It combines Eastern and Western philosophy, along with quantum physics, astrology, biochemistry, and genetics. Human Design gives you a unique blueprint for your life based on the time, date, and place of your birth. Similar to how astrology gives you a natal chart, Human Design gives you a bodygraph.

My superpower is taking complex info and breaking it down into easy-to-understand, bite-sized chunks. That is what I aim to do with my chapter in this book. If you are into astrology, spirituality, numerology, personality tests, and personal growth and development, then you are really going to dig this. If not, then try to keep an open mind and see what you can learn from this. I promise there will be a golden nugget or two for you to learn from.

At the most fundamental level, we are all energy: vibrating, buzzing, humming around. The 3D matter around us is actually an illusion (but that's a whole different conversation). Anyway, what I am getting at is that if you can wrap your head around the fact that we are all energy, you can start to understand quantum physics at a more basic level, as well as human design. We are all energetic beings with a unique energetic signature and we can leverage this power to bring more joy, ease, and flow into our lives.

Human Design is another tool for a deeper understanding of yourself. These tools, based on your unique Human Design energy type, will help you to understand how to use your energy in the most effective way possible. Your decisions will be more aligned and authentic when you start to understand how to use these tools. The cool thing about Human Design is that it isn't based on strict dogma. It's an experiment to be lived out and practiced.

One of the most important things to understand about Human Design is the energy types. There are five in total. Before you read on to the next paragraph, I want you to do me a quick favor. Pause. Put the book down for a second. Take some deep breaths, center yourself, and drop into your heart space if you can. Take a moment to get intentional with how you read about the energy types. I want you to see if you can try to figure out which one you are on your own. Follow your gut, listen to your heart, and take note of which type resonates with you the most.

There are five main energy types in Human Design: manifestor, generator, manifesting generator, projector, and reflector. Each one is unique and tells you how you should engage with and respond to the world. Read on to understand each one and to determine which one resonates the most with you. If you want to know more and do a deep dive with me on this, you can always schedule a reading with me. Before I go too deep into each type, look at the statements below to see what resonates most with you.

I am here to follow my joy and do what lights me up. My passion is my source of energy. Natural helpers, generators radiate warmth and joy. (Generator)

I like to lead and take action. I am here to bring new ideas to life. I thrive on freedom and following my impulses. Natural CEOs and leader types. (Manifestor)

I am multi-passionate and pivot easily. I may have a hard time deciding and like to change things up a lot. I am a natural multi-tasker. (Manifesting Generator)

I am the sage, the wise counsel. I am insightful and intuitive. I move more slowly than others. Natural managers and directors, others come to you for guidance and insight. (Projectors)

I am more sensitive and feel deeply compared to others. I am a natural humanitarian, concerned with peace and prosperity for all. I am like a mirror to others, reflecting themselves. (Reflectors)

Which one felt most like you? I am curious to know. Read on to find out more.

Generators are here to do what lights them up. They have access to an unlimited source of power. They are like the Energizer bunnies and can keep going and going. However, if they are not excited or lit up by what they are doing, they are likely to burn out and lose access to this energy. At the same time, once they make a commitment, they keep chugging along the path with the energy of a freight train. See the paradox here? Once a commitment is made and energy is engaged, one can't help but keep going and showing up *even if* it burns them out and wears them down. The result? Stress and burnout, spread thin. They may feel like they have no energy left to do anything else. This is why it's so important to be careful about which commitments you say yes to. Also, Generators need to learn to get out of their heads and get into their bodies to make wise decisions.

Manifesting Generators are similar to generators in that they have access to unlimited energy as well. The manifesting spin here is that they are able to bring ideas to life more quickly than the other energy types. The manifesting part does not come in less they are in direct response to their own energy. They work and think fast as well. They may lack patience. However, they also really need to learn how to slow down. Ever heard the phrase, "Slow down to speed up?" This applies here. It means that we need not rush to get our ideas out to the world, but rather respond to the opportunities that are presented to us. When we lean into this energy, slow it all down, and learn to not be in such a hurry, that is actually when we speed up our progress.

Manifestors are initiators. They are unique in that their energy type is to initiate. They have a very fierce, independent energy about them. They hate being controlled. When you are angry, that is your cue that you are not living your authentic life. They need to be informed before taking action. They need to let people around them know what they are thinking and what they want to do. Inform, then initiate. They make big waves and may cause disruption. They will find peace when they let people know things before they happen. They are here to inform and make an impact.

Projectors are like the lighthouses of the world. They are ever-steady, a beacon of light and wisdom to guide those around them. They really thrive on recognition and being seen. They don't have access to the same life force energy as the other energy types. They probably don't move and think as fast. They may need more time to figure things out. They move at their own pace and really thrive on recognition. They may not be suited for a normal 9-5 because they don't have access to this never-ending energy. Not lazy or unmotivated, just different based on this unique energy type. Knowing this will relieve any guilt or shame you may feel around not having as much energy as your family members or co-workers. A projector feels the greatest success when they feel seen and heard for who they truly are. They have a different viewpoint than most and may have a history of feeling misunderstood.

Reflectors are the rarest type—about 1% of the population. They are here to be a mirror and reflect back to the collective. They are usually deeply disappointed by the injustices of the world and may strive to find solutions to collective problems. The word "moonchild" may resonate with you, as you have a special relationship with the moon. They are here to be in awe of life. They should consider syncing their calendar with the lunar cycles. They need more alone time to recharge. They make natural humanitarians, caring deeply about the world.

Having awareness of your energy type is key here. No energy type is better or worse than the other. It's just different, and the power lies in the awareness of your unique type and knowing how to harness it to your advantage. The other really great thing about Human Design is that you can approach it like an experiment. Take the information that really resonates and start experimenting with it in your everyday life.

Another fantastic aspect of Human Design is that it encourages you to tune into your body to make decisions. Get out of your mind and into your body. So many of us get stuck in analysis paralysis and really have a hard time making decisions. I know that I have suffered from decision fatigue myself. Human Design can save the day here, as it's an easy and practical tool to use in your everyday life. Imagine when faced with a hard decision, just being able to tune into your body for the answers. The body has so much inherent wisdom for us, we just have to stop long enough to tune in and listen.

One last caveat about Human Design is conditioning. If none of this really resonates with you or makes much sense, it's most likely because of your conditioning. We are conditioned, or programmed, to act a certain way depending on the environment, families, schools, and cultures we are born into. When you are never given a chance to tune in to who you truly are and what feels right for you, you may feel lost and confused. This is because you have never been given permission to express and experiment with who you truly are. So keep in mind that our conditioning can prevent us from being able to tune in to the true essence of who we are. Awareness and intention are the keys to changing this.

I want to give you an example from my own life of how I started using my Human Design to work for me. Being a generator, my strategy in life is to respond. Unlike manifestors, who are here to initiate and take action, generators are here to wait and respond. So what does that look like in practical terms? For me, it was how I was able to change careers. After COVID and 10+ years in the medical industry, I was feeling really burnt out by the whole industry. Wanting more freedom, I decided to try to find a job where I could work remotely. That was easier said than done. I spent almost eight months job hunting and applying for various jobs on the internet. The result? One lousy interview that went nowhere. Frustrated, I decided to stop and take a break from job hunting.

About six months later, an email landed in my inbox that would prove to be the ultimate invitation for me. I was on an email list of a company that I really admired and wanted to work for. Lo and behold, they sent out an email saying they were hiring. I got so excited when I read the email because I just knew in my heart the job was mine. I was right. Out of 150 applicants, I landed the job! Do you see what happens when we stay patient and follow our strategy type? I wasted time initiating and trying to control the situation by applying for endless jobs online. My perfect invitation came via email and all I had to do was respond to it. Any other generators feel that? When we try to force life and take control too much, it usually does not work out very well in our favor. We need to learn patience and be able to have faith and trust in the universe and her divine timing. I know that it is easier said than done at times. But look back on your life and some of the biggest decisions you have ever made. Were you following your design? How did it turn out? Again, Human Design is really meant to be experimented with.

Take what resonates and leave the rest. It's an ongoing journey, not an end destination.

Recently, I had the privilege of sitting in a conference room full of hundreds of powerful and awe-inspiring women. The speaker, an expert in Vedic astrology and Human Design, said to the audience, "Knowing your Human Design is SO important for your life." She paused. "I cannot stress this enough. Knowing your Human Design is SO crucial to your life."

She went on to tell the story of her daughter and how she struggled in parenting her because she was a difficult child. She explained that finding Human Design 18 years ago was a game changer for her as it changed the way she parented and related to her daughter. I sat in that room, listening intently, captivated by her words. She is so right, I thought to myself. Her presence, her words, and her energy were such a wonderful reminder of why I am even writing the words in this book right now.

Human Design has also changed the way I approach parenting. I have learned to connect with my son on a deeper level. When I learned that he is a projector, I had this lightbulb moment where everything just clicked. He hates to be rushed. He does not have the natural access to life force energy like I do. He needs extra time to do things in his own way. Also, projectors have a huge need to be recognized. I realized just how important praise and attention are to him. I make it a point now to slow down and tune into any little thing he wants me to notice. I see now how this simple act has transformed my parenting and the way I relate to him.

Human Design is such a powerful tool that can be used to make your whole life easier and more magical. It can transform your relationships. It can make you more connected to yourself. It gives you permission to be who you really are. It will make you a better person, parent, lover, friend, and coworker. When you start to see things through the lens of Human Design, it gives you a powerful new perspective on life. You start to intuit energy types right away. You understand how to connect with others more deeply. You start living a more authentic and powerful life. And who doesn't want more of that?

I am on a mission to help empower women. To get them to WAKE up and see how powerful they really are! To reclaim their sovereignty. To say NO to the things we do not want and YES to the things that light us up. To rebel against cultural and societal norms. To have the courage and power to be who we really are. To lead more authentic lives. To have the permission to be who we truly are. To unlock your heart's full potential. To step into that next version of yourself that you really want to be, even though you may be afraid. I believe we can tap into the power of Human Design to help us create and live our dream lives, the ones we only let ourselves dream of, but feel like it may be out of reach. Human Design gives you the blueprint to take your power back and live a life you feel incredibly happy about.

I am still learning in my ongoing experiment with Human Design. Being a recovering people pleaser is not easy. I have said yes to many things in my life when I really meant no. I had been conditioned to be the good girl, the helper, the caretaker, the one who puts all needs before her own. I had learned that it was better to stay quiet, be seen and not heard, and to receive love and praise for my achievements and not purely for my being and who I was as a person. Learning to tune into my strategy type has really helped me stop these patterns. However, awareness is key when it comes to change. We can't change what we don't see.

Another deeper layer of Human Design is understanding deconditioning and learning to unlearn what we think we know. This isn't always easy. It's new and unfamiliar and the ego likes to do what keeps us safe. But sometimes safety keeps us stuck and unable to access our true power. Without our conscious awareness, we are programmed from the time we are born to act in certain ways. Our society, culture, family, schools, media, and other aspects of our environment tell us how we should think, act, and behave. It's not good or bad, it simply just is. I bring this to your attention to remind you that your programming does not define who you really are. Have you ever stopped to think and question why you believe a certain thing, follow a certain religion, or behave a certain way? Most of our behaviors and actions are unconscious, because we never stop to really think about them—until we take the time to examine them and take some inventory, we will never step into our full power.

Human Design can help with this process of deconstruction. Human Design tells us who we really are, from the moment of birth. It's a cosmic blueprint of our DNA. It does not tell you how to think, act, or behave. Instead, it gives you the freedom to use your unique energetic body to respond to what life has in store for you. When you first start learning about Human Design, it may not resonate and this is exactly why, because of your programming. If you can understand this aspect and suspend your disbelief for a minute, I bet you will be surprised at what happens when you are able to tune in to who you truly are.

If you only take one thing from reading this chapter, I hope you understand how powerful you really are. I hope you understand that we get caught up in our minds, overthinking everything. We are bombarded with negative thoughts and news all day long. We don't have to live this way. We need to get out of our heads and into our bodies. We need to learn to tune into the wisdom that's naturally available to us. There is so much wisdom there if only we are still enough to listen. Tune in to your body and learn to listen. Ask her what she is trying to tell us. Ask her what your next step is. Ask her for clarity and insight and to show you the way. Human Design can help you tune into the body's wisdom so you have an easier time making decisions in your life. It's time to change the way you have been showing up in your life. You need tools to do this and the ancient wisdom of Human Design can help you do just that. I would love to help. Book your reading here: linktr.ee/free.by.design.

MP Montigny

Founder of Anima Mundi Center
Humanitarian Emergency Specialist

www.animamundicenter.com
https://www.instagram.com/animamundicenter/
https://www.facebook.com/profile.php?id=100094493185163

Over the last decade, MP has contributed to humanitarian efforts, serving as an Emergency Coordinator and delivering aid to communities worldwide in the face of conflict, displacement, and crises. Her work in challenging environments—from Myanmar, Yemen, Beirut, Somalia, DR Congo, Central African Republic, Malawi, Madagascar, Haiti, India, and Senegal—has deepened her understanding of how compassion, contribution, and resilience can generate impactful change. Traveling through over 50 countries, MP has drawn invaluable teachings from diverse cultures. She earned certifications as a Reiki and Tianshi Master, Beyond Quantum Healer, and yoga teacher, weaving together holistic well-being and social impact. Her insights emphasize the role of selflessness in making meaningful global contributions and the power of inner connection for a purposeful life. Driven by these convictions, MP founded Anima Mundi Center, an online holistic wellness platform that inspires individuals to 'create a better world, starting with a better you.'

UNCHARTED JOURNEYS: A HUMANITARIAN'S GUIDE TO LIVING YOUR BEST LIFE

By MP Montigny

"The biggest adventure you can take is to live the life of your dreams."
—Oprah Winfrey

Introduction - Embracing Your Purpose

As I write this, sitting on a terrace with a view that stretches over a serene lake in Madagascar, I'm bathed in the warmth of sunlight that illuminates the valley below. A gentle breeze carries the sweet fragrance of flowering trees, mingling with the sounds of daily life—people gathering water, workers tending to rice fields, the hum of solar-powered radios fueling local rhythms, and the laughter of barefoot children, crafting new worlds from rocks and sticks. It's in moments like these, amidst the vibrant local life foreign to me, that I find myself reflecting on what it truly means to live a life you love. Deep down, a gentle whisper reaffirms it's all about living your purpose and finding peace within.

Looking back on the last decade, sometimes I have to remind myself that this isn't a dream—I'm really living the life I once imagined. That's not to say it's been a walk in the park. Far from it. But every single day, there's this undeniable sense of being right where I'm supposed to be, living true to myself and the path I've chosen. For more than 13 years, my life has been a bit of a wanderlust-filled adventure, dedicating myself to humanitarian work in crisis zones and exploring the world during my downtime. I've set foot in over 55 countries, each one offering its own set of lessons and helping me grow in ways I never anticipated. Diving into so many different cultures, each one as mesmerizing as the next, has filled my life with unforgettable experiences.

From traversing the dense equatorial rainforest of the Democratic Republic of Congo to following the paths of pygmies in the Central African Republic, each journey has deeply etched its stories into my soul. I've witnessed the profound resilience of Yemen's oldest Arab tribe, been touched by the strength of Lebanese people rising from the ashes of the Beirut port explosion, and been surprised by the gesture of a Senegalese woman who offered me to be the second wife of her husband to cement our friendship—which I, unfortunately, had to decline. I've been humbled by the gift of a single ring from an Indian orphan whose entire world could fit into a small box, and inspired by a young Somali woman pregnant with her first child in a displaced camp of 70,000 people, finding joy in her simple shelter because, as she said, not everyone was as fortunate. My adventures also led me to hike active volcanoes, swim alongside great white sharks, and dip in the majesty of the world's largest waterfalls.

These experiences didn't come by chance; they were the result of a conscious choice to live fully, embrace risks, live without regrets, break free from limitations, and face my fears head-on. Through my journey, I've seen the diverse realities that paint our planet—a melting pot of beliefs, cultures, and ways of living. My experiences taught me that the wonders of our planet and the diversity of its people are life's true treasures. I've witnessed firsthand the beauty of human connection, the strength that comes from community, and the joy of living in the moment. Even in regions torn by conflict, I've seen the capacity for gratitude, love, and happiness that defines the best of what it means to be human. One thing has become clear: Those seeking paradise need only to open their eyes to find it here on Earth, should they choose to.

Now, as we plan a life you love together, I invite you to consider your own life through a new lens. Take a moment to appreciate the roof over your head, the water in your tap, the people who support you, and the nature that surrounds you. It's time to shift our focus from what we lack to the abundance we already possess. If you're waiting for happiness to arrive with the next achievement or acquisition, let's break that cycle now. A life you love isn't a distant goal; it's the journey itself, filled with gratitude and appreciation for each step along the way. The present moment is where true fulfillment lies. Decide, right here, right now, that you are in love with your life. Your purpose is simply to be authentically you. If, each day, you find something to be grateful for, the life you love will unfold before your eyes.

Now that we've acknowledged that you can live the life you love here and now, let's explore how to propel you beyond your wildest dreams. How your true calling can become not just a distant wish but a tangible, achievable reality. It will take courage to navigate life's uncertainties toward your ultimate goals, but it will be oh-so worth it.

1. Assessing Your Current Life

Ever had a dream that set your heart racing with just the thought of it? A vision so captivating you'd find yourself lost in your thoughts, like playing a movie of what life could be like if that dream became your reality? Can you feel that pulse of excitement now, just thinking about it?

That was me. For as long as I can remember, I felt called to be a humanitarian. To be there, in remote corners of the world, offering a hand where it's needed most and contributing to easing suffering. I was barely 12 years old when this dream first whispered to me, not fully understanding what a humanitarian did but feeling deeply that it was my path. When asked the inevitable question, "What do you want to be when you grow up?" each time I'd shout with excitement, "A humanitarian!" And so, the vision persisted.

Yet, there was a period where the reality of my life felt a world apart from this dream. I especially remember a sweltering summer morning, standing in a crowded bus at 6:00 a.m., clinging to a strap, submerged by the scent of too many people packed too close. I was heading to my government job —one that should've felt like a lucky breakthrough, especially as a well-paying position during my first summer at university. Yet, all I was feeling was dissatisfaction with the monotonous routine, societal pressure to find security in a paycheck, and anxiety about such a predictable future. Each day left me feeling hollow, as though the job was draining me of life itself. It wasn't just about disliking the job; it was the fear that this could become my forever if I didn't make a change. Despite having all the hallmarks of a good life—health, job, friends, family, a partner—I felt an emptiness inside. I kept wondering if that was all life had to offer. Chasing societal benchmarks of success, and accumulating stuff, all while feeling disconnected from any real purpose. Were our collective destinies just endless commutes, growing frustration, and a lack of tolerance for each other?

Deep down, there was a persistent knowing that there was more to life. I yearned for a life bursting with passion, adventure, freedom—a life where I could reinvent myself, live my true desires, connect with something bigger, and make a meaningful difference. I was determined to break away from societal expectations, to escape the cage I found myself in. But the question remained: where to begin?

Exercise 1: Honesty Check

Let's start with a frank look at where we stand in our lives. Are you living a life you adore, or are there areas craving for change to truly resonate with your inner truth? Which parts of your life yearn for improvement? The goal is not dwelling on the negative but recognizing which areas of your life aren't aligning with who you aspire to be.

Examine your relationships, habits, health, work, and personality. Do they mirror the best version of yourself, the person you're destined to be? This isn't meant to discourage or breed pessimism. Rather, it's a chance to acknowledge that we often settle for "good enough" because we believe change is out of reach.

Let's dive in. Set a timer for 25 minutes, allotting five minutes to reflect on each aspect of your life, including physical, emotional, intellectual, social, and spiritual. Grab your journal and draw two columns: one for what you cherish in each area and another for what you're eager to improve. This brainstorming session is our first step into the world of self-reflection and introspection, setting the stage for the transformative journey ahead.

2. Tuning In to Your Inner Voice and Shaping Your Future

On the journey of life, our deepest dreams are like whispers from the universe, gently pushing us toward the existence we're meant to lead. These wishes often begin as soft murmurs of intuition—a gut feeling, a silent nudge toward what we're destined to achieve. They arrive unannounced, not rooted in logic or reason, but as pure, compelling desires that you might not even dare to admit to yourself. So, you tuck them away, dismissing them as impossible fantasies. Yet, these whispers are the true voice of your soul, an innate wisdom that knows you intimately and strives to guide you toward fulfilling your most profound aspirations. The desire to be a humanitarian was one such whisper for me, a calling from within that I couldn't logically justify. Being a small-town girl with a conventional life, the dream of traveling to conflict zones and mastering a complex field seemed far-fetched. Yet, the whispers wouldn't be silenced, growing louder and more insistent until ignoring them was no longer an option.

It's important to understand and recognize that our minds often disconnect us from our intuition. To override this programming, let's pause to ponder our purpose. Find a quiet spot, sit down, and contemplate the following:

- What drives you throughout the day? What activities do you gravitate toward in your leisure time?
- In which domains do inspiration and motivation effortlessly arise for you?
- In which contexts do you perceive your efforts as valuable, and in which contexts do you find yourself seeking direction?
- Reflecting on your emotions, what insights do they offer about the journey you're on?
- Do you have a clear sense of purpose or mission? If it seems absent, is there a moment in the past when you felt connected to a deeper calling?
- What intentions have you set for your life, and in what ways do you live out these intentions each day?

This initial reflection on what you aspire to achieve and on your core values is a profound way to connect to yourself. Your purpose should resonate so deeply that it becomes tangible; not just words, but a truth you feel in your very being.

Now that the mind is leaving space for our intuition, let's move further!

Exercise 2: Diary of Your Future Self

Here we will venture into the future. Prepare your journal, and take a moment to close your eyes, breathing deeply in and out. Date your first entry 20 years ahead. Begin by describing a day in your best possible life in great detail. Imagine waking up in your ideal reality—where you are, who you're with, your morning rituals, and how you feel. Elaborate on your day, touching on your career, relationships, hobbies, and health. Delve further by exploring the senses and emotions associated with your best life: How does the morning air smell? What sounds fill your home? What's the texture of your clothes? What emotions are you experiencing throughout this day? Joy at your work? Love and connection with family and friends? Pride in your personal accomplishments?

I encourage you to do this exercise over several days, as each session will reveal new insights and perspectives worth considering. After a week, review your diary and observe the common thread uniting your dream life. What are your newfound priorities? What's most important for you? What is the main feeling you are aiming for? This is your purpose, unfolding before your very eyes.

Now, shift your viewpoint and write a letter from your future self to your present self. What guidance do they offer? What insights or encouragement do they share about navigating to this best life? From here, start thinking about actionable steps that edge you closer to this envisioned existence. What minor adjustments can you implement today? Hold on to this thought; we'll delve deeper shortly.

By writing detailed narratives, you're not just fantasizing about your desired life; you're living it through the eyes of your future self. I can't even remember how many times I did this exercise, and how many profound discoveries I've made. This approach not only clarifies your true priorities but also the central endeavor you seek to achieve. By doing so, I've personally uncovered how I want my day to unfold, what my aspirations are, and what new habits I want to implement in my life. It's a powerful way to visualize your goals and motivate you to act toward making them a reality, supported by the wisdom and encouragement of the future you.

With this introspective visualization, we're laying the groundwork and starting to link vision with action, reclaiming the life that may have been obscured by societal expectations, the pressure to conform, and the trap of comparison.

3. Cultivating an Empowering Mindset

Before we go any further, defining the actionable steps toward cultivating a life you love, it's crucial to first confront our belief system, ensuring we're not the architects of our own limitations to reaching our fullest potential.

You may have been tuning out your inner voice, the one steering you toward what you truly desire, simply because you lack belief in its feasibility. I know I sure did! Deep down, there might be a lack of self-trust, or perhaps fears and doubts casting shadows over your faith in the possible. Questions such as "What if I fail?" "What if I lose everything?" or concerns about others' perceptions might plague you. Worries over financial stability, or the thoughts of your family, friends, and society can weigh heavily. Doubts like, "Am I good enough?" and "Do I have what it takes?" might echo in your mind. You might convince yourself that you're content with what you have, fearing that striving for more could lead to loss or disappointment. How can change occur if you feel immobilized? I can't tell you how terrified I've been…leaving everything behind to move from country to country, by myself, to go into some of the world's worst crises of the last decade. I mean, what the heck was I thinking? One thing was for sure—not going was even more scary to me. Living life as I knew it was petrifying me even more than not trying.

It doesn't mean that I'm dismissing these apprehensions as unfounded. Instead, I encourage a shift in viewpoint. Adhering to the same old patterns will only yield the same results. As the saying goes, "To get something you've never had, you have to do something you've never done." This means releasing the grip of those limiting beliefs and becoming the version of yourself that aligns with your highest aspirations. This path toward a life filled with love and fulfillment requires us to shed our outdated selves and constraining patterns that have held us back. We need to redefine ourselves, tuning into our inner wisdom, and transcending our fears and limitations.

Exercise 3: Shifting Your Beliefs

To start the process of breaking free from limiting beliefs, a powerful exercise that worked for me was vivid visualization of the consequences of clinging to these restrictive thoughts.

First, find a quiet space where you can focus without interruptions. Close your eyes and deeply imagine the trajectory of your life if you allow these limiting beliefs to guide your decisions. Picture the opportunities you'd miss, the dreams you'd forsake, and the person you'd become, stagnating on this unfulfilled path. Take the necessary time to really picture in detail what your life would be, and what regrets you would hold on to. What long-term consequences does holding onto these beliefs cause? Think of today, in a year, in five years, later in your life.

Then, shift your visualization to a life where you've conquered these beliefs—envision the achievements unlocked, the joy experienced, and the expansive growth of your true potential. Imagine all that you will accomplish without these limitations. See yourself surpassing your fears, breaking free from old patterns, and unlocking your deeper desires.

By comparing these two divergent paths in detail, you'll awaken a profound realization of what's at stake, motivating a compelling drive to embrace change and pursue a life unbounded by past constraints.

4. Setting Achievable Goals and Taking Inspired Action

Before I started my bachelor's degree, I quite often daydreamed about my life as a humanitarian. I saw myself overseas, dressed for the field, working in communities that needed help. These visions prompted questions: How do I get there? What actions should I take? What skills, knowledge, and experiences are necessary to achieve this vision? This led me to research the qualifications needed for humanitarian work, which included earning a master's degree in a relevant field, gaining volunteer experience, becoming trilingual, developing management skills, and acquiring travel and international work experience.

I started by breaking down my dream into specific, measurable, and time-bound goals, then crafted an action plan to achieve them. This pathway, spanning over many years, required consistent effort, but was guided by the belief that each step, while challenging, was a joyous part of the journey toward my ultimate objective.

Exercise 4: Goals That Support Your Purpose

Having connected with your life's vision in the second exercise, it's time to establish actionable targets that will propel you forward. This exercise, while straightforward, demands careful consideration so you can set goals with timelines that are both ambitious and realistic, to gauge progress.

In your journal, note the primary purpose identified in your Diary of Your Future Self visualization. Below this, list five or six concrete, achievable goals that bolster this mission. For instance, if your purpose is self-love, you'll need specific goals to monitor your advancement:

My purpose: To be the best version of myself.

My goals:

- Daily meditation and journaling.
- Twice daily, shift my thoughts from expectation to gratitude.
- Treat my body as a sacred temple, engaging in physical activity at least three times a week.
- Avoid the evening news, focusing instead on nurturing my inner peace with inspiring stories.

- Engage once a month with groups that embody positivity and transformation.
- Support a cause I'm passionate about through time or donations each month.

Align your actions with the core reasons behind your goals, as this alignment fuels your long-term motivation. Feel free to refine your goals as you evolve and uncover new insights on your path to self-discovery.

5. Nurturing Growth and Personal Evolution

My journey has been deeply enriched by planning ambitious adventures and refining my mindset, yet in my opinion, the cornerstone of my achievements has been a commitment to personal growth. Throughout my life, I've tried a variety of experiences that can seem easy on the surface, but that were highly challenging for me. From the emotional challenges of living in war-zone countries, the physical health challenges of traveling alone to remote, undeveloped countries, the spiritual challenges of immersing myself in meditation retreats, the professional challenges of launching a business, and even the mental challenges of spending a year in Thailand to heal myself from the post-traumatic stress disorder suffered in war zones.

These endeavors were made possible through dedicated self-improvement efforts. Reaching your desired life doesn't happen by accident; it's the result of actively seeking out the knowledge, resources, and growth necessary to achieve one's aspirations. A profound realization I've come to is captured in the saying, "What I know is that I know nothing." This acknowledgment opened my eyes to the vastness of what I had yet to learn, especially when confronted with new cultures, conflicts, and perspectives that challenged my preconceptions. For instance, the year I started my business, I knew I was starting from the bottom, and I had so much to learn and experience. I moved to a secluded island to concentrate, enrolled in an online business course, hired a business coach, attended meditation and detox retreats, participated in weekly mastermind sessions, and joined webinars and seminars led by industry leaders. I surrounded myself with individuals who shared my ambition, eager to absorb their wisdom, acquire new skills, and establish daily rituals that kept my objectives clear and my spirit aligned.

Exercise 5: Your Personal Growth Plan

It's your turn now! Select approximately three approaches to implement for your personal growth and choose a timeframe in which to make it happen. Here are some examples, but feel free to come up with your own:

- Map out a specific learning journey tailored to the skills you need.
- Seek out growth opportunities that resonate with your personal and professional aspirations, which may include workshops, seminars, books, and courses.
- Connect with a mentor or coach who can guide you through your journey.
- Find an accountability partner or join a mastermind group to share and support your goals.
- Engage in practices that nurture your mental and emotional well-being, such as meditation, yoga, or journaling, to maintain clarity and focus.
- Incorporate daily reminders of your purpose, such as a vision board, affirmations, inspirational quotes, or personal letters.
- Experiment with new experiences that push you out of your comfort zone to enrich your perspective and enhance your adaptability.

- Cultivate a community of supportive peers who share your aspirations and values. This could be through joining clubs, online forums, or local groups where you can exchange ideas and encouragement.
- Reflect regularly on your progress and recalibrate your goals as necessary. Personal growth is an evolving process, and what serves you at one stage may need adjustment as you develop.
- Study the paths of those who've achieved your goals and learn from their strategies.
- Maintain a journal to document your progress and insights.
- Celebrate your achievements, no matter how small, recognizing that each step forward contributes to your larger vision.

By integrating these strategies into your life, you create a dynamic environment for continuous learning and self-discovery. It's crucial to remember that personal development isn't a race to the finish line but a nonstop journey. Each day offers a new chance to grow and become a better version of yourself, using every success and setback as a stepping stone toward your ultimate goals. This commitment to growth not only brings you closer to realizing your dreams but also enriches your life with depth, meaning, and fulfillment.

While investing money into your growth can be useful, the real value comes from investing your time and commitment. Luckily, the abundance of resources available online, many of which are free or low-cost, means that financial limits don't have to hold us back. In essence, as you engage in personal growth, you're no longer yearning for a distant future; you're actively shaping it through your own evolution.

6. Cultivating Energy and Wellness

I'm no fitness icon, but once upon a time, I did lead aerobic classes— ah, those were the days. Today, though, I want to reflect on a phase in my life when my energy hit rock bottom, as I now understand it mirrored my internal disarray. It was a time when everything felt off—my job, daily routines, relationships, like a burnout from neglecting self-care.

This is when holistic wellness became a game-changer for every facet of my life. It's not necessarily about hitting the gym or eating right; it's about achieving harmony between mind, body, and spirit. Our untapped energy reservoirs are linked to our overall state of being. Unaddressed emotions, for example, manifest physically. Our surroundings influence us too, with negativity or toxicity draining our vitality.

When I made the firm decision to pursue my desired life with all of my focused attention, I found myself gradually distancing from individuals, activities, and situations that no longer resonated with my path. It was an instinctive move to safeguard my well-being. Growth demands transformation, and as we evolve toward our true selves and the life we envision, it becomes essential to shed the old—the habits, the people, and the practices that no longer fit our journey.

Exercise 6: Learning to Say "No"

This one's a challenge, especially for the people-pleasers, the ones always prioritizing other people's needs above their own. It's time to practice saying "no" to what no longer serves us. I'm not broadcasting about becoming self-centered but about prioritizing our needs and goals. Saying "yes" should come from genuine desire, not obligation or fear of societal backlash.

So much of our time and energy can be consumed by unwanted commitments, leaving us frustrated and drained. I don't want you to be isolated from your community but to choose engagements that energize rather than deplete you.

Here are a few examples of how to gracefully decline:

- "I'm really trying to focus on personal time this week, so I'll have to pass on [event]."
- "I wish I could help, but I'm spread too thin at the moment."
- "I appreciate the offer, but I just can't fit it into my schedule."

Remember, it's okay to say no. Being assertive yet courteous in your refusal frees up your energy for what truly matters to you. Over time, you'll see this as an act of self-love, crucial for maintaining your energy and overall well-being.

7. Navigating Uncertainty with Openness

A few years back, I found myself in Yemen, amidst a challenging mission close to the conflict lines, where nightly bomb vibrations were a grim reminder of the hazardous situation. During this time, a colleague and friend was tragically killed in another conflict zone, marking a low point in my career. I still can't hold back my tears while writing these lines and reliving the tragedy of the situation. Struggling with burnout, trauma, and the physical manifestations of stress, including severe adult acne and loss of hair, I questioned my path and considered a drastic career change.

Then, an unexpected turn: A job posting in Thailand seemed like a sign, a potential new direction. However, that opportunity quickly slipped away, and I spiraled back into doubts about my future. Shortly after, an unusual offer appeared for a remote consultancy role supporting humanitarian efforts in Myanmar, requiring a base in the same timezone—meaning…Thailand. The rest is history. This shift to remote work, initially unthinkable, turned out to be the unexpected answer I hadn't dared hope for. I ended up living there for longer than any other missions I've been on, and the peaceful and secure environment allowed me to tune into myself and make drastic life changes that led me to a new path. Everything happens for a reason, you might say.

This journey taught me the power of remaining open to unforeseen possibilities. Clinging too tightly to one path or method can close off avenues that might lead us to our desired state of being in unexpected, yet fulfilling ways. Trusting in a larger plan, staying flexible, and receiving the surprises life throws our way. The universe has a funny way of unfolding, often reminding us that our best-laid projects are mere suggestions. As the saying goes: "If you want to make God laugh, tell him your plans."

Exercise 7: Guiding Principles for Embracing Life's Unpredictabilities

Consider this more of a guide for your path to a life you love. Regularly reflect on and integrate these fundamental principles.

1. **Enjoy the Journey, Not Just the Destination**: Life is a collection of milestones, not a single achievement. True happiness comes from within, not from external gains. Focusing solely on the destination can blind you to the value of the present. Learning to appreciate your current position can lead to a more satisfying journey, often with results that exceed your initial aspirations.

2. **Redefine Success**: Chasing after specific outcomes, such as wealth, based on arbitrary benchmarks is like navigating without a map. Shift your perspective to embrace broader, more meaningful objectives—seek a sense of abundance and the freedom to live your life fully. This mindset fosters openness to a wider range of fulfilling achievements, concentrating on the feeling of your desires rather than on rigid endpoints.

3. **Value Experiences Over Outcomes**: Prioritize life-enriching experiences over the pursuit of material possessions. This approach encourages you to fully engage with the process, savor each moment of learning, and remain open and adaptable to the twists and turns of life. By prioritizing experiences, you transform your life into a deeply rewarding expedition, where every step is an opportunity for joy and self-discovery.

Conclusion: Your Roadmap to True Self-Discovery

As we close this chapter on building a life you're genuinely excited about, let's take a moment to revisit the steps. We've combined connecting within, dreaming the impossible, maintaining a constructive outlook, taking meaningful actions, improving yourself, and embracing change into a holistic strategy for life. We've also looked at the appreciation of the present moment, the value of each step, and the strength found in flexibility.

Picture yourself at a crossroads today, recognizing your inner power and the endless opportunities ahead. Now is the time to take that initial leap, no matter how small, toward a life of purpose and passion. Let this guide be your compass as you explore the depths of your potential, reawakening that intuitive spark within that leads to true happiness and fulfillment.

Reconnecting to your authentic self is all about stripping away layers of conditioned beliefs and hearing your true essence. You're in charge here, with each belief carving out your path. Choose those that lift you up, opening doors to new possibilities. I challenge you today to step into your greatness and shake off the fears and doubts holding you back. Have faith in your extraordinary potential and let that belief illuminate both your path and those around you. The future is shaped by the choices you make now. Stay present, let go of resistance, and ride the wave that brings you closer to your dreams.

Ultimately, a life you love is uniquely yours. By holding true to what matters most and remaining open, you create experiences that define a life well-lived. Cheers to the journey ahead, filled with learning, evolving, and the pure joy of being unapologetically you.

Trish Gleason

The World Wellness Show, LLC
Host and CEO

https://www.linkedin.com/in/lovetaxfree
https://www.facebook.com/loveworldwellness
https://www.instagram.com/lovetaxfree
https://www.worldwellnessinterviews.com/
https://www.youtube.com/@theworldwellnessshow

Trish Gleason is a dedicated host and the founder of The World Wellness Show, LLC, a streaming TV Show now broadcasting in 137 countries on FENIX TV, a platform committed to sharing educational health and wellness information through insightful interviews with holistic doctors and other specialists. Born and raised in the Midwest USA, Trish has always had a profound passion for helping and educating others.

With a successful career as a wealth advisor spanning 29 years, Trish's path took an additional direction when she discovered a deep interest in the holistic methodologies practiced by many of her doctor clients. This newfound passion led her to launch her own TV show in 2018, where she has been engaging in conversations with medical professionals to spread awareness and knowledge about holistic health practices.

Beyond her professional endeavors, Trish is a loving grandmother to fifteen-grandchildren and proud mother of three children. Her dedication to making a positive impact by creating a paradigm shift from sick care to wellcare shines through everything she does."

READY, SET, REVERSE:
NEW DISCOVERIES THAT TURN BACK
THE CLOCK OF AGING

By Trish Gleason

**THE WORLD
WELLNESS**

The sky's the limit *no matter your age*—but only if you've got your mind and health. Laura Ingalls Wilder, author of the *Little House on the Prairie* series, began writing at age 65. Grandma Moses, a folk art icon who began painting in 1938, became a worldwide icon and was on the cover of *Time* magazine at age 78. Campbell's Soup… Does that sound familiar? Joseph Campbell became rich and famous for inventing condensed soup as we know it today at the age of 78. Your life is ahead of you so make the imaginable come true with good health—a LIFE you love. It is essential to recognize the fundamental importance of prioritizing our health to "Plan a LIFE You Love." A strong and vibrant body and mind not only enable us to pursue our passions and dreams, but also serve as cornerstones of a fulfilling, joyful, and, hopefully, LONG life.

In 2024, the life expectancy for people in the United States is 78.9 years, and is expected to be 81.9 in 2054. Longevity is trending upward, as life expectancy in the US was 75.62 in 1994 & 71.5 in 1944. By creating a paradigm shift from sick care to well care and spreading the knowledge you learn from this chapter, with *The World Wellness Show*'s educational messages we can, collectively, make an exponential difference globally. When we neglect our well-being, we risk missing out on the endless opportunities and experiences that life has to offer. Our health is not just part of having a life we love, it is the foundation necessary to be able, physically and mentally, to live life to the fullest.

As the host of an internationally streaming program, *The World Wellness Show*, broadcast in 137 countries on FENIX TV, I've had the pleasure of interviewing many internationally recognized holistic doctors and researching how best to plan to live a life I love. I'd like to share the many secret findings with you in this chapter with quotes from doctors, on the show through interviews, and in the Facebook group "HUSHLadies," where women around the world share their secrets about health, wellness, and anti-aging. Assisting others in their growth and learning has always been a personal passion of mine. I am happy to mentor you by engaging with additional doctors, researching, and finding extremely valuable knowledge needed for us to live a longer, happier, more fulfilled, and beautiful life. My mentorship and providing doctor interviews will not cost you a nickel, but you will have to invest some time into watching the interviews and educating yourself, then applying what you learn.

"As we age, it is not uncommon to have discouraging, emotional feelings and thoughts such as "life is passing me by," or, "I may be at the end of the road." Although I'm a super motivated, vibrant, and uplifting person, it has been tough at times to get a grip on the fact that so much of life is behind me, and it has been a struggle to make sure that I look to the future with a positive outlook and a purpose in life. Most likely everybody has had these unsettling thoughts when they glance through old photos, etc. The right diet and exercise have helped me gain more stamina and mental fortitude in a big way. Another factor that has helped me gain immense drive is re-evaluating my purpose in life. A valuable purpose can guide life decisions, influence behavior and mental clarity, create goals, and really give us a sense of direction."
—Trish Gleason

"The University of Minnesota's research explains that a "purpose" can influence physical health to live longer, protect against heart disease, prevent Alzheimer's disease, handle pain better, and lead to better relationships. Having a purpose is the difference between making a living and making a life." A study from *Psychology Today* found that having a purpose can alter your perception in life and correlates directly with health, wealth and happiness.[1]

No matter your age, your whole life is the future, so create the best possible outcome. What we eat and how we exercise are the ROOT of our good or bad attitudes, energy levels, desire or passionate outlook levels, sleep habits. and so much more—it is nearly everything needed to live a great life. My resources and the knowledge gained by interviewing doctors will provide you with incredible, holistic discoveries to turn back the clock to help you have better mental fortitude, feel younger, look younger, be healthier, have more energy and a better outlook on life, and ultimately have more life to live. Go to FENIXTV.app to view complete interviews and learn more from other holistic specialists.

Planning for a life you love may not be as difficult as you think. If you've got your health in good order and a purpose, the sky's the limit. Can you imagine the changes to your and your family's lives with the potential to reverse dementia, prevent Alzheimer's, or even grow new pathways in your brain? Looks like it is possible! As the host of *The World Wellness Show,* I am privileged to share with you the many "secrets" I have uncovered from the doctors I have interviewed. Traditionally, we get sick then we treat the sickness, whereas reversing this customary "plan" and having a pre-sickness approach will make all the difference in the world. I've compiled my findings of key factors to

---

[1] https://www.psychologytoday.com/us/blog/making-sense-chaos/202109/3-crucial-discoveries-about-purpose-in-life

turn back the clock of aging—proactive, holistic approaches to being healthy and reversing the damage done to our bodies. In this chapter, we provide education on the newest discoveries related to turning back the biological clock, exploring a multitude of perspectives from dozens of internationally recognized holistic and regenerative medicine doctors. Each of these medical experts has dedicated their careers to a proactive approach to health, wellness, and anti-aging with emphasis on longevity, vitality, and reversing the effects of time on the human body. Through their collective discoveries and endorsement of diverse approaches, we can help the world unlock the keys to not only slowing down the aging process but also rejuvenating our bodies from within. This includes potentially reversing dementia, preventing Alzheimer's, and much more.

Let's begin a new era together

Together, let's create a paradigm shift from SICK CARE to WELL CARE. With the rapid advancement of medical research and breakthroughs in understanding the complexity of aging, we are ready for a proactive approach, rather than a reactive approach, to begin a new era—one where the prospect of reversing the damage done to our bodies is available and ready for your embracing. Through these interviews, we gain invaluable education about the latest scientific discoveries, innovative treatments, and practical lifestyle modifications that hold the potential to turn back the hands of time.

What are you looking for?

From exploring the transformative power of regenerative medicine to cutting-edge nutritional strategies, my guests can help you gain the knowledge to master the art of biological rejuvenation. Do you have a family member with dementia, chronic dizziness, or arthritis, or do you want to find out how to be proactive and prevent you and your loved ones from becoming sick? Our esteemed panel of doctors shares their expertise on a wide range of topics, including:

- Reversing disease
- Reaching delta sleep and it's importance
- Fascia's impact on aging and more
- Hormones and the impact on longevity
- Intermittent fasting and how it can prolong your life
- Digestion and your health
- Food and the impact on your body and life's longevity
- Cellular regeneration
- Hormone optimization
- Stress reduction and how stress causes 90% of illnesses
- Telomere lengthening to reverse cellular aging
- Epigenetic modulators to reverse age-related changes
- Mitochondrial health to improve functions and reduce oxidative stress to rejuvenate at a cellular level
- Stem cell therapy and the newest discoveries
- Microbiome and aging with gut microbiome interventions, like probiotics, to restore more youthful microbiome
- Epigenetic clocks—measuring changes in DNA to potentially intervene to reverse the aging process and the role of exercise in reversing the aging process
- iPSC—cellular programming with ability to reprogram adult cells back into a pluripotent state, rejuvenating cells and tissue
- Senescence reversal—potentially reversing age-related tissue dysfunction
- Brain-gut connection and longevity

(Go to FENIXTV.app - The World Wellness Show - for complete doctor interviews)

"Be proactive, be knowledgeable BEFORE something bad and irreversible occurs that could jeopardize living life to the fullest." —Trish Gleason

The collective knowledge of the doctors interviewed on FENIXTV.app—*The World Wellness Show* offers a holistic approach that empowers individuals to take charge of their own health and embrace the possibilities of a rejuvenated tomorrow. Whether you are seeking ways to regain youthful energy, enhance cognitive function, or simply improve your overall well-being, the knowledge shared by these experts will serve as a foundation for your personal journey to reverse the biological clock.

Things are different now than in years gone by, and the prominent holistic doctors mentioned in this chapter can provide much-needed insight to educate you on the "upgrades" toward better health in 2024 and going forward. As children, we were often fed and taught a balanced meal of fried chicken, pot roast, and mashed potatoes with lots of butter, milk, gravy, bread, and more. This was our standard dinner and, worse yet, this was similar to meals at schools, hospitals, and everywhere else…and probably still is today. After I watched three documentaries (below), my diet immediately became 90% plant-based. I hope this is going to happen to you as well after watching the programs. I have many close friends and relatives who are plant-based and I just really didn't know the benefits. More importantly, I did not know the ramifications of eating the way we were told to eat all of our lives. The ramifications to the environment and to our bodies are devastating. Do you remember the food pyramid you were taught in elementary school? Meat, cheese, milk, and bread were a category on their own.

I was at the Department of Health recently getting a duplicate birth certificate for my daughter, and I noticed on the bulletin board they had a sign saying, "Is milk good for you?" It had a chart showing the difference between cow's milk, coconut milk, soy milk, and almond milk (I personally started using a pea milk called Ripple with my plant-based cereal and it is fabulous tasting). The cow's milk was not the winner. You have to wonder why we are told to drink cow's milk and then there are contradictory signs at the Department of Health. Since I've started the plant-based eating style, my mental clarity has increased dramatically, my energy level is up, my sleeping habits are much better, my skin is more beautiful, I have lost weight (not counting calories or watching carbs but eating only during an eight hour per day window for intermittent fasting), and my body functions are working great.

Doctor Interviews:

Interviews were conducted with the following doctors and very powerful excerpts are quoted below. These complete interviews and many other interviews may be viewed free on FENIXTV.app—*The World Wellness Show*, LLC:

- **Dr. Steven Anton, Gainesville, FL:** University of Florida Dept. of Physiology and Aging, Professor at UF Institute on Aging (international expert on intermittent fasting). Intermittent Fasting Science & Longevity
- **Dr. Paul Finucan, Naples, FL:** Alternative Health and Healing Center & Weight Loss Done Right Clinic. One of the largest holistic clinics in the US. Regenerative Medicine and How it Impacts Longevity

- **Dr. Daniel Fenster, New York City, NY:** Director of the internationally recognized Complete Wellness Clinic has had the privilege to treat royalty, diplomats, and sports elites with holistic and pain treatments for over four decades.
- **Dr. Clint Steele, Portland, ME:** TRUCHIRO—creator of the NeuroInfiniti. How Stress Can Cause 90% of Sickness
- **Dr. Patrick Porter, New Bern, NC:** Creator and CEO of BrainTap Technologies, international speaker and expert on sleep. How Sleep Impacts Your Health
- **Dr. Tom Lankering, Basalt, CO:** Veteran brain-based wellness TV talk show host of 21 years Biohacking Discoveries to Prevent Sickness, CEO Lankering Chiropractic & Brain Based Wellness, Honorary Council Member—*The World Wellness Show*

<u>**Dr. Stephen Anton, Gainesville, Florida**</u>, has been a global leading authority on intermittent fasting, obesity, metabolism, and aging for over 20 years. He is a professor and Chief of the Clinical Research Division at the University of Florida's Department of Aging and Geriatric Research and has conducted many studies on intermittent fasting and its impact on longevity and is recognized as an international expert and keynote speaker. Department of Physiology and Aging, College of Public Health and Health Professions, College of Medicine, University of Florida, Clinical Research Division UF.

"Currently, there are no established dietary or behavioral interventions for extending a healthy lifespan or "healthspan" in at-risk older adults that can be widely implemented. Based on evidence from preclinical models, there appears to be strong potential for interventions that directly target the biology of aging and thus have the potential to improve overall wellness. Specifically, lifestyle interventions, such as intermittent fasting or exercise, that assist individuals in activating their metabolic switch, and thus shift the body from storing fat to using it for energy, have the potential to activate biological pathways that extend a healthy lifespan. While genes and the environment definitively play a role in our health, the choices we make about our diet, exercise, and sleeping patterns can have a tremendous effect on our level of wellness. Each of these activities is critical to your wellness, and when combined in a specific way can extend your healthspan. The key is becoming aware of what your body and mind need and getting into a healthy routine to look and feel your best!"

—Dr. Stephen Anton
Contact: 352.273.7514

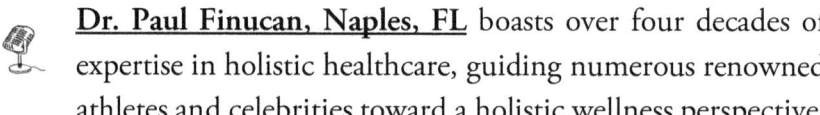 **<u>Dr. Paul Finucan, Naples, FL</u>** boasts over four decades of expertise in holistic healthcare, guiding numerous renowned athletes and celebrities toward a holistic wellness perspective. As the proprietor of three holistic clinics in Naples, Florida, he focuses on a wide array of services, including injury and illness prevention and recovery, organic skincare, weight management, and more. Dr. Finucan emphasizes holistic approaches that consider the interplay of hormones, stem cells, exosomes, and much more with the ultimate goal of reversing biological age for a happier, healthier lifestyle. Known worldwide for his proficiency in holistic medicine and as a leader in stem-cell treatment, he emphasizes his holistic approach to preventing diseases and surgeries by evaluating your entire brain and gut connection, boosting stem cell production, and presenting a comprehensive wellness strategy.

"We are all derived from stem cells inherited from our parents, which have the remarkable ability to divide and differentiate into various types of cells such as skin cells, liver cells, and more. Stem cells play a crucial role in the body's repair and regeneration processes. At birth, approximately 1 in 10,000 cells in a baby are stem cells, while in a 60-year-old, this number decreases to 1 in 10 million, indicating a decline in stem cell population with age.

Stem cell research has been ongoing for four decades, with significant advancements made in the past nine years. Exosomes, which are signaling molecules one-ten-thousandth the size of a stem cell, have emerged as a novel approach for stimulating repair and activating nutrition, and can be administered via injection into the abdomen. Anecdotal evidence includes a skeptical older doctor in their 70s who initially doubted the effectiveness of stem cells until discovering that platelet-rich plasma (PRP) therapy facilitated their own blood regeneration, contrasting with the use of Wharton's jelly extracted directly from a newborn's umbilical cord, flown in overnight on dry ice for immediate application to areas like the knee or hip.

Utilizing different therapies alongside stem cell treatments can enhance the stimulation of targeted areas, leading to improved outcomes for various conditions. To explore potential treatments, one can search for a specific disorder followed by "exosomes" or "stem cells" online. It is essential to emphasize awareness and proactive measures for longevity, happiness, and overall well-being as longevity concerns everyone. A patient's success story of avoiding hip replacement through stem cell therapy and red-light therapy, leading to a restored ability to rollerblade at 70 years old, exemplifies the transformative potential of such regenerative treatments in promoting a more youthful biological age."

– Dr. Paul Finucan
Contact: DrFinucan@gmail.com; www.mynapleschiropractor.com; 239.592.7767

Dr. Daniel Fenster, New York City, NY In his 30+ years of practice, Dr. Fenster has treated many professional athletes and celebrities. He was on the medical staff of the USA Maccabiah Team, the second-largest sporting event in the world after the Olympics. Dr. Fenster is an internationally recognized chiropractor and has flown all over the world to treat royals and diplomats. He is an innovator of the Integrated Model and has helped many patients by combining Acupuncture, Chiropractic, Massage, Nutrition, Functional Medicine, Psychology, Physiatry, Physical Therapy, and Yoga. In addition, Dr. Fenster is the host of the *COMPLETE WELLNESS* radio show on WABC Radio, the host of the upcoming podcast *BEYOND BIOHACKING*, a sought-after lecturer in stress management for businesses and corporations, and the author of three books: *Free Your Fascia*, published by Hay House, *CRYOTHERAPY— The Secret To Staying Young*, and soon to be released *UPRIGHT—The Body Language of Success*.

"Highlighting the crucial significance of fascia in preserving good health and its impact on longevity, there is a growing emphasis on understanding the role of fascia. Emphasizing holistic approaches and proactive wellness strategies like chiropractic adjustments, stretching, yoga, and staying hydrated plays a pivotal role in supporting the health of fascia and overall well-being.

The interconnected nature of the body is underscored, with every part playing a role in overall health. Fascia, being a pervasive network throughout the body, is crucial for optimal functioning and is gaining recognition for its impact on well-being.

As famously quoted by Benjamin Franklin centuries ago, *"An ounce of prevention is worth a pound of cure."* Creating a paradigm shift from sick care to well care can make a profound difference in lifestyle and longevity.

Nutrients like amino acids, vitamin C, collagen, electrolytes, and magnesium are identified as important for fascial health, with hydration being a key factor. Factors like vitamin D intake are highlighted as significant for health, with many individuals potentially not getting enough of this essential nutrient. The standard range for vitamin D is 30, with the recommended optimal range being 50 to 60. Insufficient vitamin D levels can impact your mood, immunity, and various other aspects of health. While the direct relationship between vitamin D and fascia remains uncertain, it is crucial for overall bodily function and well-being.

Research into the complexities of fascia is ongoing, indicating that there is much more to learn about its role in the body. Understanding and caring for our fascia may play a crucial role in maintaining a healthy and balanced body. Upon waking in the morning after a period of no fluid intake, it is advisable to hydrate immediately by drinking water. To replenish electrolytes without increasing sodium intake, using products like LMNT electrolytes is suggested, particularly for individuals without high blood pressure.

The pervasiveness of fascia in the body is a topic that still lacks comprehensive understanding. Recent research cited in my book from Helene Langevin, Director of the Osher Center for Integrative Medicine at Harvard Medical School and Brigham and Women's Hospital, particularly on page 69, suggests that early stretching may have potential benefits in reducing cancer risk by decreasing inflammation in the body through the manipulation of fascia. The detrimental effects of poor posture and alignment, which can lead to restricted and dehydrated fascia, inflammation, and discomfort, are highlighted. Engaging in proper stretching routines and maintaining well-functioning fascia can contribute to a longer and healthier life.

Based on extensive experience gained from interacting with patients around the world who often invest significant sums in treating their illnesses without always achieving desired outcomes, the importance of proactive health and wellness practices over reactive approaches is emphasized. Cultivating a positive mindset and focus can facilitate creating a more constructive environment compared to dealing with negativity. Finally, the detrimental effects of smoking on health are underscored as a significant concern.

Smoking has a detrimental impact on your fascia, polluting both your fascia and the entire body, leading to long-lasting harm. To achieve relaxation, consider breathing exercises instead. Sugar and alcohol also negatively affect your fascia: Sugar breaks down and damages your fascia. Therefore, it's advisable to opt for foods low in sugar and minimize sugar intake as a preventive measure. Neuropathy, weakness, numbness, and pain from nerve damage, often associated with diabetes, are challenging to reverse once they occur, emphasizing the importance of proactive health choices to avoid such conditions. Alcohol, being a form of sugar, shares similar detrimental effects, as ethanol acts as a neurotoxin and negatively affects brain neurotransmitters. Minimizing alcohol consumption is recommended for improved health.

Pain and inflammation in the body are potential indicators of fascial issues. Implementing changes in nutrition, staying hydrated, seeking guidance from a holistic chiropractor, and quitting smoking can help address such problems. Proper daily vitamin intake may contribute to preventing dementia, underlining the significance of proactive health measures. Healthy fascia, located just beneath the skin, can support skin health, potentially reducing the appearance of wrinkles. While there may not be a direct link between fascia and organs, the interconnected nature of the body underscores the importance of fascia in maintaining organ health. Understanding the role of the immune system, such as the PD-1 immune checkpoint, in reducing cancer risk is crucial, with stretching potentially playing a role in limiting cancer development. Taking charge of your health proactively can have far-reaching benefits for your overall well-being and quality of life".

—Dr. Daniel Fenster
Contact: Dr.Fenster@completewellnessnyc.com 212.737.9000

Dr. Clint Steele, Portland, Maine, Co-founder of Brain Based Health Solutions and owner of a revolutionary biohacking cognitive brain and nervous system assessment technology, NeuroINFINITI, enhancing mental performance by optimizing brain function and efficiency. With over 31 years of experience as a brain-based holistic doctor, he leads cutting-edge brain-based coaching globally, emphasizing holistic mental performance and education as an esteemed international speaker.

"According to numerous experts, including the NIH, over 90% of all disease is due to stress. Let me explain by presenting this in a very easy-to-understand way. I'll start by first asking a question: What *coordinates* every function in your body? Of course, the brain. The way it does this is through this simplified two-step process.

1. The brain must perceive the environment.
2. The brain then uses that perception to determine how it's going to change the physiologic function of the body.

For example, the fire alarm goes off in the building right now. Your brain perceives that fire alarm as stress. This stress leads the brain to coordinate the function of your body so you can escape the burning building. Things like increasing your heart rate, your breathing rate, your muscle tension, changing neurotransmitter and hormone release, and more. We call this survival mode.

Let's say, however, that this fire alarm was a false alarm. You go back into the building, the stress is gone, and now your brain perceives the environment as safe, leading to what *should* be a slower heart rate, breathing rate, lower muscle tension, a change in neurotransmitter and hormone release, and more. We call this healing mode.

As you may know, your brain cannot be in healing mode and survival mode at the same time. Your brain also doesn't know the difference between fire alarm stress and relationship, financial, fear, or worry stress. It's all just stress to the brain. Based on how your brain learns to deal with stress, starting while in your mom's womb based on how your mom dealt with stress, you begin to create a neural pattern, and, good or bad, that pattern becomes the "norm." This all happens 95% of the time at a subconscious level.

So, if your brain's "norm" is stuck in survival mode, thinking the building is on fire, how well can it coordinate the digestion of food? Sleep? Reproduction? What would happen to blood pressure? Inflammation? Pain? Anxiety?

This is the foundational cause of disease.

The good news… Thanks to a term known as neuroplasticity, these patterns can be changed, leading to not only better health but a better life!"

—Dr. Clint Steele, DC, CSCS
Contact: 207-240-4908

Patrick K. Porter, New Bern, NC: Creator of BrainTap Technologies and International Keynote Speaker and authority about sleep. Four decades of advocating for holistic health and wellness has given Dr. Porter a goal to help better a billion brains. He is the author of the award-winning bestseller *Awaken the Genius, Mind Technology for the 21st Century* and has hosted his own show on WNIS radio in Norfolk, Virginia, for ten years.

Sleep and Longevity

Sleep is crucial to longevity. Your body is a finely tuned machine and sleep is an integral part of it. When you're sleeping, your body uses that time to repair and cleanse the brain of toxins that accumulate during the day. It's your body's way of hitting the reset button to tackle the challenges of the next day. When you don't get good, quality sleep, you're setting yourself up for a host of problems including increased risk of heart disease, obesity, and a weakened immune system. This doesn't bode well for a life of longevity. If you want to live a long and vibrant life, make sleep a priority.

It's been said that getting less than six hours of sleep is akin to "suicide." That may be a bit sensationalistic, but when it comes to longevity, quality sleep is a must. During a typical night's sleep, our bodies go through various stages including deep sleep and REM sleep. These stages are all vitally important for rest but also to regulate our neurochemistry. Inadequate sleep interferes with the production of neurotransmitters such as serotonin and dopamine, which then impairs our ability to cope with stress and negatively affects brain function. Chronic lack of sleep can have a long-lasting impact on our mental health and longevity. It's not just about waking up feeling refreshed. It's about maintaining good health in our minds and bodies for life.

—Dr. Patrick Porter
www.braintap.com

Dr. Tom Lankering, Basalt, CO An award-winning "Chiropractor of The Year" for Colorado State, a brain-based and bioenergetic doctor of 40 years, a holistic doctor and former 21-year TV host for a wellness show in Colorado, Dr. Lankering has vast insight on your digestion and food and how it impacts your health.

Dr. Lankering explains: "Healing your gut is a priority for potentially reversing your biological clock. Your gut produces more serotonin than your brain, has more nerve cells than your spine, and 80-90% of your immune system is in the gut. This is why it is so crucial that you protect your gut. Protecting your digestive system starts with good digestion. Your brain and gut have a direct connection via the vagus nerve. If your brain is happy then you will have a healthy gut. The opposite is also true; an unhappy gut leads to an unhappy brain. We live in a toxic quagmire today. The food we eat can create hormone disruptions, clog up your liver, and can cause obesity and immune challenges, including allergies. Irritable bowel, Crohn's, leaky gut, gastritis, diverticulitis, and more may be CAUSED by food not digesting properly. If the body cannot digest proteins, it often leads to arthritis; if it cannot digest carbohydrates, it can cause diabetes, and when it cannot digest fat, we can get cardiovascular disease. Make sure your gut has the proper digestive enzymes to digest your food. Digestive enzymes are available as a supplement. It is also important to keep your gut balanced with proper flora and probiotics.

- Chew your food
- Eat foods that do NOT have toxins and are especially NOT GMO (Genetically Modified)
- Drink plenty of water
- Raw plants have digestive enzymes. Cooked plants do not.

If your food is not digested properly, you will not get the proper nutrients. This may lead to various diseases. It is important to support your parasympathetic nervous system (the vagus nerve). Many people are in a fight-or-flight state (stress mode). This is the sympathetic nervous system. By balancing these two systems, one can optimize one's digestive system."

—Dr. Tom Lankering
Contact: dradjust@sopris.net; 970.927.9900 or 970.379.9063

Plan a Life You Love is an amazing resource to help you be successful in every area of your life. I am confident that the most valuable part of this book and the most integral part of your being successful and happy in life is to Plan a LIFE You Love by first and foremost *making your health your primary concern.*

In my decades-long tenure as a financial advisor, I can confidently assert that the true pillars of well-being—health, happiness, and love—far outweigh the significance of wealth. Through my extensive experience, I have witnessed numerous cases in which individuals possessed vast fortunes yet lacked the crucial component of good health and happiness. While financial stability is undeniably important, it does not compare to the profound impact of one's health and emotional well-being.

I recognize the importance of financial success, but I have also seen, far too often, how an excessive focus on wealth can lead to unhappiness and even depression. True fulfillment stems from nurturing your physical and mental health first and foremost by balancing diet, regular exercise, and mindfulness practices. When you prioritize your well-being as discussed in this chapter, your thoughts become clearer, your life more enjoyable, and your outlook brighter. Taking a journey of self-discovery and exploring the power of a proactive approach to health and wellness can add years to your life.

By educating yourself about health and wellness solutions and options and maintaining a solid physical and mental state, you create the resilience and determination needed to pursue financial success. Your great energy empowers you to approach wealth creation with the purpose of creating and taking opportunities to generate income effectively. Success begins with health and wellness education and applying a proactive approach to health and wellness.

Personal Suggestions: I strongly suggest watching four documentaries streaming on Netflix most released in 2023-24 and visiting the following Facebook group.

- Live to 100: Secrets of the Blue Zones
- You Are What You Eat—A Twin Experiment
- What the Health
- Poisoned, The dirty truth about food
- HUSHLadies: https://www.facebook.com/groups/hushladies1/?ref=share_group_link

All five resources are fantastic and have truly transformed my life. *What the Health* offers a glimpse, a shocking look, into the processing of our food. The Facebook group consists of 1,200 women from various parts of the world, sharing health and beauty secrets such as utilizing fermented rice water or onion juice for promoting hair growth, snail mucus to rid eye wrinkles, and many more valuable insights for women. Prepare to be inspired, informed, and empowered as we uncover the transformative strategies that can help us defy the limitations of time. **My key takeaways from the expert interviews in this chapter and suggestions I apply to my life are:**

1. Wake up with a <u>glass of water</u> to drink next to bed. Our bodies are very dehydrated upon waking. Dr. Fenster describes how our fascia plays a crucial role and water is the most important factor.

2. Only <u>fall asleep with a clear mind</u>. Do not fall asleep without meditating a bit, going through the day's events, and clearing your mind ending with good thoughts. BrainTap light, sound, and vibration technology assist with sleep issues. Deep delta sleep is when our brain rebuilds neurotransmitters. It's best not to watch the news as often it is negative, with the mental turmoil causing an inability to enter delta sleep.

3. <u>Intermittent fasting</u>, eating in six-eight hour periods only. Dr. Anton describes how allowing our food time to digest creates a more efficient body and most likely longer lifespan.

4. <u>Reduce stress</u> since it causes up to 90% of all illness. NeuroINFINITI/Dr. Steele's assessments and training modules identify your baseline and provide six-minute-per-day online testing to train your brain to reduce stress and relax.

5. <u>Stem cell therapy</u>, especially the cells from umbilical cords, is working miracles for people with ailments and people who are healthy but want to increase longevity. Dr. Finucan explains not all stem cells have good results and that it is important to use high-quality stem cells.

6. <u>Brain-gut connection</u>—Dr. Lankering explained how the gut produces more serotonin than the brain, that the brain and gut are connected through the vagus nerve, and how important it is to eat a more plant-based diet. If the body cannot digest proteins, it often leads to arthritis; if it cannot digest carbohydrates, it can cause diabetes, and when it cannot digest fat, we can get cardiovascular disease. Taking pro- and prebiotics daily will help gut function.

Together, let's unlock the potential for a vibrant, healthy, and longer, more purposeful future ahead concentrating on having a truly proactive approach to health, wellness, and anti-aging.

Trish Gleason, Author
Host - The World Wellness Show, LLC
help@theworldwellnessshow.com
www.TheWorldWellnessShow.com
(352) 871 7171 or (404) 444 0905

JOIN THE MOVEMENT!
#BAUW

Becoming An Unstoppable Woman
With She Rises Studios

She Rises Studios was founded by Hanna Olivas and Adriana Luna Carlos, the mother-daughter duo, in mid-2020 as they saw a need to help empower women worldwide. They are the podcast hosts of the *She Rises Studios Podcast* and Amazon best-selling authors and motivational speakers who travel the world. Hanna and Adriana are the movement creators of #BAUW - Becoming An Unstoppable Woman: The movement has been created to universally impact women of all ages, at whatever stage of life, to overcome insecurities, and adversities, and develop an unstoppable mindset. She Rises Studios educates, celebrates, and empowers women globally.

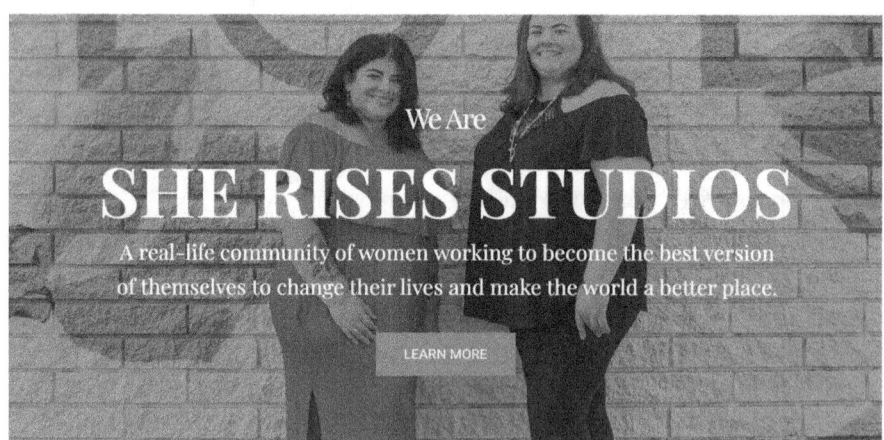

Looking to Join Us in our Next Anthology or Publish YOUR Own?

She Rises Studios Publishing offers full-service publishing, marketing, book tour, and campaign services. For more information, contact info@sherisesstudios.com

We are always looking for women who want to share their stories and expertise and feature their businesses on our podcasts, in our books, and in our magazines.

SEE WHAT WE DO

OUR PODCAST

OUR BOOKS

OUR SERVICES

Be featured in the Becoming An Unstoppable Woman magazine, published in 13 countries and sold in all major retailers. Get the visibility you need to LEVEL UP in your business!

Have your own TV show streamed across major platforms like Roku TV, Amazon Fire Stick, Apple TV and more!

Learn to leverage your expertise. Build your online presence and grow your audience with FENIX TV.
https://fenixtv.sherisesstudios.com/

Visit www.SheRisesStudios.com to see how YOU can join the #BAUW movement and help your community to achieve the UNSTOPPABLE mindset.

Have you checked out the *She Rises Studios Podcast?*

Find us on all MAJOR platforms: Spotify, IHeartRadio, Apple Podcasts, Google Podcasts, etc.

Looking to become a sponsor or build a partnership?

Email us at info@sherisesstudios.com